ENDORSEMENTS

There are crucial questions to answer about the fairness and effectiveness of an inspection culture that ignores or undermines the professional vision of teachers in their own schools, or tries to homogenise philosophies of education in the name of inappropriately standardised outcomes. This analysis of one significant but not unique example of the problems that can arise with school inspections is an uncomfortable but necessary challenge to current educational orthodoxies.

> **Dr ROWAN WILLIAMS,** former Archbishop of Canterbury, University of Cambridge

This report demonstrates a striking level of ethical corruption – a state institution that claims to have identified an instance of inadequate safeguarding involving bullying, and then takes action in a way that has damaged the bonds of relationship between pupils, parents and teachers – an action that epitomises the inappropriate use of force, i.e. bullying. OFSTED's relationship with Steiner Waldorf education makes no more sense than setting the Sandhurst military academy to evaluate the Royal Ballet.

> **DENIS POSTLE,** psychotherapist, writer and film-maker

Ofsted embodies and propagates a culture of malignity, fear and intimidation. This is one example of its misfeasance – indeed, malfeasance. It is unfit for purpose. It should be abolished and replaced by a body akin to the former HMI, Her Majesty's Inspectorate of Education, or some such body whose culture and aims should, while being inspectorial and evaluative, be supportive rather than suppressive.

> **DAVE HILL,** Emeritus Professor of Research in Education, Anglia Ruskin University, Cambridge and Chelmsford; Visiting Professor of Education, Middlesex University, London, and the National and Kapodistrian University of Athens, Greece

This report explains in close detail how the prevailing culture of standard-isation, surveillance and control at all levels of education is fundamentally destroying the UK education system. This oppressive and punitive system of audit is wholly inapplicable to any idea of what education actually is. If the situation at any school were as grave as Ofsted claims in this case, then it behoves such an inspectorate to provide real engagement with teaching and support staff, parents, carers and pupils, not the current controlling stric-tures. It is tragic what is happening to education before our very eyes, as this report examines. Something must change before it is finally too late.

> **KARIN LESNIK-OBERSTEIN,** Professor of Critical Theory and Director of the Graduate Centre for International Research in Childhood: Lit-erature, Culture, Media (CIRCL).

It seems extraordinary that Ofsted, with its insistence on protocol as the answer to everything, does not itself have a well worked-out protocol for how it will assess institutions meeting educational need by other means.

> **PROFESSOR DAME MARILYN STRATHERN,** Social Anthropologist, editor of *Audit Cultures*

Richard House's surgical analysis of OFSTED's condemnatory report on Wyn-stones (Steiner) School throws into high relief two questions, the implica-tions of which have profound significance for the educational experience of thousands of pupils and teachers throughout our land:
 (i) what constitutes a 'good education'?; and (ii) What does it mean to speak of the professionalism of teachers? Dr House's 'counter-report' demonstrates that OFSTED is ill-equipped to address, let alone provide cogent answers to, these questions. Its adherence to some of the worst aspects of our account-ability culture results in the seemingly dogmatic application of an ideology totally at variance with an understanding of education informed by world-views embracing very different concepts of the person and of learning.

> **PROFESSOR BRIAN THORNE,** Emeritus Professor of Counselling, Uni-versity of East Anglia, and former Professor of Education, College of Teachers

This report demonstrates not just the bullying and oppressive regime generated by Ofsted but its growing unfitness for purpose. Ofsted's view of 'a good education' has become a narrow rigid focus on educational outcomes that works against rather than with teachers' professionalism. It has also led to the sidelining of creativity and critical thinking skills, and a reductive understanding of pedagogy and learning processes. As this counter-report convincingly demonstrates, an inflexible tick-box mentality that rigidly pre-defines what a 'good' school should look like is no way to assess the rich complexity of schools such as Wynstones.

PROFESSOR DIANE REAY, University of Cambridge

Over the last 40 years or so, central government has exhibited deep distrust in values-based educational philosophies. Pervasive and, frequently, explicit, this distrust is articulated at the levels of curriculum, institution and teacher. The ensuing surveillance systems evidently impose a narrow and impoverished educational 'philosophy' on those within its field of vision. House's counter-report exposes the absurdity of an inspection regime that emphasises bureaucracy, audit, subject expertise, cookie-cutter curriculum and high-stakes summative assessment making judgements about an institution with a focus on holistic child-centredness, humanism and the joy of learning.

PROFESSOR WILL CURTIS, University of Warwick

When school standards serve those who set them rather than the schools themselves, when freedom is sacrificed to performativity, when creativity is relegated and accountability elevated, something profoundly wrong happens in our schools. OFSTED did not merely close down Wynstones; it committed an act of violence against an entire community. In the late 1990s, Alexander Neill's Summerhill school successfully battled OFSTED's attempts to close it down and it will soon be celebrating 100 years of service to democratic education. Wynstones must follow suit! Being different is not a threat; it is an honour bestowed to those who fight for ideals.

Dr SPYROS THEMELIS, Associate Professor, University of East Anglia

This book not only subjects the audit-driven Ofsted inspection approach to much-needed critical scrutiny, but also refreshingly opens up an equally needed examination of both the safeguarding culture that so dominates policy-making, and the negative unintended consequences that a narrowly legalistic application of 'safeguarding' generates.

PREM SIKKA, Professor of Accounting and Finance, University of Sheffield (Emeritus Professor, University of Essex)

*To the country's brilliant teachers, who labour
under unnecessary and demoralising regimes
of compliance and fear*

PUSHING BACK TO OFSTED

Safeguarding and the Legitimacy of Ofsted's Inspection Judgements – A Critical Case Study

Richard House

InterActions

Published by InterActions, Stroud UK
interactionspublishing@outlook.com

ISBN 978-0-9528364-2-1

Distributed and available to order from
Wynstones Press
Stourbridge UK
www.wynstonespress.com
info@wynstonespress.com

Wynstones Press is an independent separate business entity, and as such is not related to the Wynstones School written about in this book.

Layout and cover design by Denis Postle ARCA

Printed in the UK

CONTENTS

EXECUTIVE SUMMARY

In early 2020, Wynstones Steiner School of Whaddon, Gloucestershire (est. 1937), was closed by order of the Department for Education, following a damning inspection report from England's Office for Standards in Education (Ofsted). The 21–22 January Ofsted inspection report on which the closure was based (see https://tinyurl.com/upzdmx2) reads like a horror-story of educational malpractice and ineptitude (referring to the depiction of the school, not to the inspection report per se).

In this book, after outlining a summary of the main characteristics of Steiner Waldorf schooling and how it differs from the mainstream, a comprehensive 'counter-report' to Ofsted's closure report on Wynstones School is presented, quoting verbatim from Ofsted's own report with a detailed forensic analysis of both the internal logic, or otherwise, of the pretexts given for Ofsted's judgements, and also situating those judgements within a wider paradigmatic discussion of what are often incommensurable and incompatible educational and pedagogical worldviews.

The analysis focuses in particular on questions of safeguarding, safety culture and professional responsibility; school culture, leadership and Ofsted's impact on the school's teaching body; pedagogy and differing learning paradigms; and Ofsted's overarching Audit Culture 'proceduralism'. At the heart of the book is its lengthy Chapter 2 on safeguarding and its vicissitudes, which opens up essential questions about the negative unintended consequences that an unthoughtful, narrowly proceduralist application of safeguarding ideology gives rise to.

The book concludes with a detailed justification of the view that the closure of the school was unjustified and grossly disproportionate; that the safeguarding problems caused by the precipitate closing of the school dwarf any safeguarding issues that were present in the school, pre-closure; that the forced, unwarranted school closure has traumatised over 250 children and their families; and that the Department for Education and Ofsted must be held to account for this gross injustice, with its affront to parental human rights to choose the education of choice for their children.

An appendix presents a detailed analysis of the multiple impacts that the school closure had on parents, based on a special questionnaire survey carried out on parents' experiences. The many parents who completed the fact-finding questionnaire deserve our appreciation and gratitude for their courage in committing to paper the often highly traumatising experiences they have had to endure. Their stories provide a testament to the degree of devastation that is caused by the fateful decision to forcibly close a school without any consultation with, or accountability to, the parents and children affected.

WHO IS WRITING THIS REPORT?

I am an academic (retired former senior university lecturer in Education Studies, and in Psychology and Psychotherapy); a social science researcher (Ph.D.); a writer (with 13 books to date, and countless papers and articles, many peer-reviewed in academic journals); a Chartered Psychologist (BPS-registered); a former counsellor-psychotherapist (for 17 years, 1990–2007); and a trained Steiner class and Kindergarten teacher, who worked as an early-years leader and teacher with Norwich Steiner School and the Norwich Steiner Initiative for 10 years (1998–2007).

All of these various and diverse professional 'hats' will therefore be informing what follows. I share this information not to 'flash credentials', or to play 'the expert card', but merely so that readers can see the kind of background that is informing what follows in what I am calling this 'counter-report'.

DISCLAIMER AND ACKNOWLEDGEMENTS

This report is written in a strictly personal capacity, as an educational consultant and academic, and is in no way connected to, or written on behalf of, any school, including Wynstones.

An anonymous reviewer (an emeritus professor of education) helpfully suggested ways in which an earlier draft of this document could be re-organised to make it more readable and digestible; and as a result I have given close attention to style and accessibility, with less jargon, repetition and rhetoric in the text. My warm thanks to this reviewer, and to several other colleagues who have made useful comments on an earlier draft.

Thanks also to Professor Saville Kushner of Edge Hill University for writing an excellent, context-setting foreword to this book, and to Kevin Avison for his prescient Afterword. I am also grateful to the eminent educationalists who have kindly read and endorsed an early draft of this book.

Any errors, omissions, intemperances or excesses in what follows are my own.

FOREWORD

Professor Saville Kushner

Edge Hill University, Ormskirk, UK

Author of *Evaluative Research Methods: Managing
the Complexities of Judgment in the Field (IAP, 2016)*
and *Personalizing Evaluation* (Sage, 2000)

Gene Glass is one of the foremost theorists of educational assessment. In 2003 he republished his seminal 1977 paper – 'Standards and criteria' – arguing that the urgency of challenging cut-off scores and performance against absolute standards was intensifying:

> I feel that in education there are virtually no absolute standards of value.
> 'Goodness' and 'badness' must be replaced by the essentially comparative
> concepts of 'better' and 'worse'. […] Absolute evaluation in education – as
> reflected in such endeavours as school accreditation and professional licensing
> – has been capricious and authoritarian.

If anything, the problem has become yet more intense. Glass goes on:

> I am confident that the only sensible interpretations of data from
> assessment programs will be based solely on whether the rate of
> performance goes up or down. Interpretations and decisions based on
> absolute levels on performance on exercises will be largely meaningless,
> since these absolute levels vary unaccountably with exercise content and
> difficulty, since judges will disagree wildly on the question of what
> consequences ought to ensue from the same absolute level of performance.

In the report in this book, we have concrete evidence of variation among judges. Ofsted attempts to make judgements against apparently absolute standards ('good', 'worrying', 'unsafe', 'poor behaviour', 'serious risk', and so on). Their judgements rely upon an appeal to common assumption, repetition, and political authority. Richard House counters that these are terms whose meaning is plastic and contextual – 'what constitutes valid "evidence"?', he asks. To concerns that children may be unsafe since universal standards of safeguarding are absent, House says, 'this leaves completely out of account the contextual professionalism and professional responsibility of teachers and staff' – and their disciplined 'thoughtfulness'.

The question of valid evidence is central to Glass's argument, since educational criteria that underpin judgement are vulnerable to variation in time, space and the nature of a task. Cronbach (1979), another of the USA's pantheon of leading 'measurement experts', argued, while renouncing his hitherto psychometric testing work, that in education, 'all generalisations decay':

> At one time a conclusion describes the existing situation well, at a later
> time it accounts for rather little variance, and ultimately it is valid only as

history. The half-life of an empirical proposition may be great or small. The more open a system, the shorter the half-life of relations within it are likely to be.

As the Ofsted inspector moves from one school to another, the generalisations they carry in their kit-bags are already in decay – 'in need of improvement', 'satisfactory'. The journey from a State school to a school defined by alternative educational philosophies like a Steiner school brings more rapid decay, for such a school is a far more 'open system'. Even were we to believe the unlikely claim that occasional parachutists into such complex milieu as classrooms can begin to apprehend educational quality, Ofsted inspectors are not given the freedom to engage with a school context and its particularities, and their methods are ipso facto invalid. A classroom today is not the same world as that classroom yesterday or tomorrow; a classroom 'here' cannot be like a classroom 'there'. What Ofsted methodology fails to account for is the paradox that all classrooms are recognisable and familiar across the world, but that two classrooms on the same corridor in a school are worlds apart.

Ofsted has learned this lesson before – sometimes painfully. One prominent example was their debacle at Summerhill School – possibly the most open of educational 'systems' we could find, and, thereby, not subject to any imported generalisation or standard. In 1999 an inspection team whose draft report was broadly favourable to Summerhill was sent back to produce a less favourable report. Nuances were altered and the school was damned, bound for closure. A subsequent judicial review (in which I played a part in generating evidence of student views) found the inspection process invalid, including for an unwarranted dismissal of the particular philosophy of the school. This, from Stronach (2005) who led the academic team evaluating the Ofsted inspection:

> The Nuffield team comprehensively inspected all of the OfSTED data relating to Summerhill. It became clear that the aims of the school were neglected in the 1999 Inspection. There were four main reasons for this.
>
>> First, it was evident that HMI did not value these aims: 'The school's values and ethos are a very significant barrier to real improvement' (School Profile);' '[a] root cause of these defects [in attainment] is non-attendance at lessons.' The school allows the pupils to mistake 'the pursuit of idleness for the exercise of personal liberty'.
>>
>> Secondly, it was because they did not care to investigate these values in practice. For example, only 1 of the 54 lodged HMI Observation Forms addressed out-of-class learning. The school as a learning community was neglected. There is no evidence from the teachers and pupils at the school that the HMI paid any attention in their questions to broad, developmental aims. Indeed pupils reported that the most frequent question was 'how often do you attend lessons?'.
>>
>> Thirdly, it was because HMI wanted to 'ensure that all pupils are fully engaged in study across a broad and balanced curriculum'. The school had therefore placed an 'unacceptable burden of responsibility' on the pupils, tantamount to an abdication of 'professional responsibility'.
>>
>> Finally, the Inspection 'Framework' made these biases in terms of the focus of the Inspection inevitable. In offering 18 evaluative categories of judgement, only four related at all to the School's central aims (see paragraph above). Accordingly, the HMI report devoted eleven sections to teaching/formal curriculum and only three to matters of spiritual, moral, social and cultural development.

Echoes here of Richard House's analysis, below, of Ofsted's failure to apprehend the Steiner philosophy and the professionalism of Wynstones teachers.

> During the course of our evaluation of the Ofsted inspection (in support of the legal team), one of the Summerhill 'kids' made this observation of Ofsted inspectors, showing again the legitimate variation in judges' values:

> I don't know how they did it, how they managed to miss the point so badly. Maybe subconsciously they want Summerhill to fail because they missed the chance to come here themselves. Maybe they should come and finish their childhood so they can leave everyone else to get on with theirs.

And another, critical of Ofsted methods –

> I would like them to ask: 'What do you do in your free time?' 'Why is it so important for you to be at Summerhill?' 'why is it so important to you that Summerhill doesn't close down?' – all these kind of questions. Lessons for me isn't the main priority because lessons aren't the only skills you need for life. You need social skills, a wide range of things that you need to know like apart from what you learn academically.

Under Ofsted inspection conventions, school students are passive subjects of the conditions in which they are, in fact, agents. One of the key flaws in Ofsted methodology is that inspectors jealously guard judgements of educational quality, and deny access to teachers, parents and students (whose views may be taken into account, but subject to veto).

These criticisms of Ofsted are common, and have been for some years. Yet the system survives and persists. One reason is that we seem to find it hard to think of alternatives. There seems to be common justice involved in the pretence that we can easily measure one school against another, against a common measure. This school's 'goodness' can be measured against another school's 'badness'. But there are alternatives.

Quality assessment of university research departments in British universities involves self-assessment via panels of reviewers drawn from the research profession. These assessments are made against common criteria, but allow for expression of the research culture of each submitting department. The assessment is based on self-reporting. There are numerous flaws to this process which might contest its validity, but it has accomplished a high degree of consensus amongst Higher Education professionals. A more sophisticated approach is taken in Sweden, where universities select partner universities (at home and in other European countries) against which to benchmark their activities. Again, there are common standards, but those standards are used as a focal point for each university to share experience as a provocation to self-evaluation.

What is attractive about the Swedish example is that, unlike the UK Research Excellence Framework analysis, key interactions are collegial conversations across institutional boundaries, and are conducted in the language of the practitioners involved. Of course, this system, too, has its flaws – but no matter. These are useful starting points for considering alternatives. The value of allowing schools to abandon their commercial/competitive isolation and to rediscover themselves through collaboration with partner schools is a return to the years of, for example, Teachers Centres, where the kind of movement and improvement spoken of by Gene Glass (quoted above) were generated through conversation and exchange, with the sharing of experience and a resulting shared experimentation.

By far the most attractive and elaborate system of school evaluation, however, is found in New Zealand, where school review (not inspection) is conducted as a collaborative, developmental partnership between reviewers and teachers (Lai & Kushner, 2013). Two- or three-day visits to a school – based on a pre-prepared self-assessment – are run as an extended workshop. The school is asked what would be most useful for the reviewers to explore as a route to improvement and tackling acknowledged weaknesses. This is a developmental exercise, and the process is characterised by constructive questioning and negotiation. School Review is not accountability based, but oriented to change.

This shift from accountability to change is the key departure from the Ofsted model of school inspection. Ofsted can be, and frequently is, challenged for its politicisation, its flawed methodology, its unethical practices and punitive outcomes; but perhaps its most egregious failing is this focus on accountability. Ofsted requires schools to look backwards so as to verify what they have done, to be risk-averse given the potentially punitive outcomes, to speak in the language of compliance and justification. Models like the Education Review Office in New Zealand reach towards a quite different approach in which schools look ahead to what they might be, and how they might respond to social change, to embrace risk, to speak in the language of aspiration and to be openly self-critical rather than pathologically defensive, as Ofsted demands.

I do not know Wynstones Steiner School. I once supervised an empirical study of the Steiner School movement and I was both admiring of and critical of what I learned and saw – probably in equal measure. We must be critical of all schools, on behalf of students and their families and the professionals within, all of whom need to know the scale and nature of their accomplishments with this continuing experiment in knowledge. But not least on behalf of the citizenry which is, even in a liberal democracy, always vulnerable to backsliding on historical gains in rights and equity.

But my student's critique treated the school as sui generis, which is how I treat all the schools I study. We invented no abstract criteria to import, nor did we seek to dissolve the uniqueness of the Steiner school in the soft soap of made-up standards. That way we learn from those who, like us, try and fail in our educational endeavours. Ofsted inspectors were experimentalists in their past life, insisting, themselves, on their uniqueness, on their courage in taking risks and their resilience in learning from their mistakes. Dare not one to claim success. I was critical of the Steiner school in its own terms. All schools have the right to be represented in their own terms, and all observers bear the duty to do that representation. Does this imply reinventing the wheel every time we enter a school and a classroom? Yes, indeed it does. Is this feasible? Yes. Look at New Zealand. Is this a comfortable message for Ofsted? No. But why should schools like Wynstones bear the burden of Ofsted's lack of courage, imagination… and independence?

References

Cronbach, L. J. (1975). Beyond the two disciplines of scientific psychology. *American Psychologist*, 30 (2): 116–27.

Glass, G.V. (1977). Standards and criteria. *Journal of Educational Measurement*, 15: 237–61.

Lai, M. & Kushner, S. (eds) (2013). *A Developmental and Negotiated Approach to School Self-Evaluation* (Vol. 14). Bingley, UK: Emerald.

Stronach, I. (2005). Progressivism against the audit culture: the continuing case of Summerhill School versus OfSTED. University of Illinois: Urbana-Champaign: paper presented to the First International Congress of Qualitative Inquiry, 4-7 May, under the title of 'On Her Majesty's Disservice: The Government Inspector and Summerhill School' (conference website: http://www.qi2005.org).

PART I

Setting the Scene for Schooling Paradigms in Conflict

These schools are differently constituted and the teachers are working under different conditions.... Anyone who enters the Waldorf School for the first time without having made himself conversant with certain vital considerations through the study of the pedagogy and literature of the School, is setting foot in an unknown land. He cannot possibly do justice to the School and its work unless he is ready to study thoroughly and without prejudice the special characteristics of its psychological and educational basis, and also to try to understand, in its deepest and innermost being, that peculiarly individual life which even the State authorities recognise in it. Without this, no one can form an objective impartial judgment of a school which differs so vitally from the ordinary schools.[1]

F. Hartlieb, *The Free Waldorf School at Stuttgart Founded by Rudolf Steiner*, Anthroposophical Publishing Co., London; Anthroposophic Press, New York, 1928, pp. 5–6

[1] The author of this book, F. Hartlieb, was the State inspector of the first Stuttgart Waldorf school in 1926, and he wrote this book about his experience of the school, published two years later in 1928.

INTRODUCTION

When my only tool is a hammer, the world becomes a nail.

ABRAHAM MASLOW

This book contains a detailed critical analysis of the judgements made in Ofsted's Inspection Report on Wynstones Steiner School, Whaddon, Gloucestershire, on 21–22 January 2020 (#115793), which was used by the Department for Education as the pretext for closing the school virtually overnight.

The decision to enforce the closing of a school by government edict is something that thankfully happens extremely rarely in the education world; and on those miniscule number of occasions when it does occur, one expects to find clear and proportionate grounds underpinning and justifying the fateful closure decision. The knock-on effects and collateral impacts of forcing a school to close are so enormous that where there exist any doubts as to the probity of such a decision, they demand a full and detailed investigation, to ensure that a grave injustice has not been perpetrated on a school's children, families and teachers.

As an educationalist, psychologist and retired university senior lecturer in Psychology and Education Studies, who cares passionately about children's right to a humanistic, holistic education, and for their parents' right to choose such an education for their children, I have major concerns about the recent forced closure by the Department for Education of Wynstones School. As a trained Steiner teacher myself, I was very concerned to hear of the closure of a school that I know has nurtured and inspired many thousands of young persons since it was founded in 1937. I therefore eagerly read the Ofsted inspection report which was used as the pretext for closing the school.

What I found was, frankly, shocking. My reading of Ofsted's report, as revealed in the detailed analysis in this book, discovered a litany of unsubstantiated assertions and highly questionable, if not fallacious, judgements. I also found that Ofsted's worldview about what constitutes 'a good education' was being used as the metric by which to judge an educational approach – Steiner Waldorf education – that differs in principled, fundamental ways from the metric that was being inflexibly deployed to assess and, ultimately, condemn the school.

What follows is in places a tough, unrelenting read; but I believe it has been essential, as a matter of historical and public record, to subject the Ofsted closure report to a forensic, line-by-line analysis, in order that its multiple shortcomings are fully articulated, and the scale of the injustice perpetrated against Wynstones School fully exposed.

In addition, this 'counter-report' (as I am calling it) is only in places written as an orthodox academic paper. Based on a careful questionnaire survey of parents' experience of the school closure, my colleague Richard Brinton and I know about the degree of outrage, anguish and suffering that has been caused by this forced school closure. To write with complete 'academic detachment' about what has happened to this living school community in this most human of stories would feel singularly inappropriate. However, I have been careful not to allow my feelings about what has happened to drown out *the rational, academic case* in what follows – and I have well over 100 cited references from the academic literature at the end of the book.

In holistic Steiner Waldorf education, a core aim is *to integrate head and heart*, and mind and body, rather than keep them artificially split asunder at the behest of an outmoded Cartesian consciousness; and what follows should very much be read with this in mind. Indeed, this latter point speaks directly to the issue of *incommensurable (learning) paradigms and worldviews*, which will form a key focus in this book.

I believe that it is vitally important that the shortcomings of Ofsted's closure report, and the way in which that report has been used to close a successful and much-loved school, are made known and freely accessible across the education world. For the questions discussed in what follows are by no means confined to Steiner Waldorf education (which just happens to be the vehicle for this book), but are relevant to any educationalist and concerned citizen who believes that our children's schooling experience should be a freeing, creative-artistic, imaginative and above all humanising one, rather than one that instrumentally 'inducts' children into a status quo that privileges materialism, consumerism and narrow Audit Culture values and practices. I return to these vital issues throughout this book.

I hope that the way in which I have refuted Ofsted's judgements in this book will empower others in comparable circumstances to find their voice, and the capacity *to speak truth to power* where power is being used in ways that are demonstrably unjust, and which cause suffering to those victimised by such abuses.

A final note on coding. In what follows in The Analysis section (Chapter 2 onwards), and for ease of reference, verbatim quotations from the Ofsted report under analysis here are in **bold**; and my own commentary on the report's findings are in regular type. This will make it immediately obvious as to who is saying what in what follows.

CHAPTER 1

Steiner Waldorf Education: Features and Key Differences from Mainstream Education

Receive the children with reverence; Educate them with love;
Relinquish them in freedom.

RUDOLF STEINER

In the History of Ideas, one of the most abiding mysteries of the twenty-first century is just how one of its most inspired, original and wide-ranging thinkers and seers, Rudolf Steiner, is so comparatively little recognised, or even known of, in the range of disparate fields on which he has had, and continues to have, such a profound influence. The author of over 30 books and the deliverer of over 6,000 lectures in his lifetime, his full collected works come to an extraordinary 350 volumes; and his lasting legacy includes uniquely innovative 'impulses' in fields as wide-ranging as curative education and social therapy (the world-renowned Camphill Communities); biodynamic agriculture (precursor of organic agriculture); holistic (anthroposophical) medicine; architecture and design; the arts (Eurythmy, painting, speech and drama); organisational consultancy; ethical banking and finance – and, of course, education.

Steiner was a widely respected philosopher and scientist in his day around a century ago, and his then singularly unfashionable *holistic* approach to human experience was many decades ahead of its time. It is only now, when so-called 'new paradigm', post-modern epistemologies and cosmologies are beginning to undermine the *Zeitgeist* of a narrow technocratic modernity and scientism, that Steiner's remarkable insights – which both incorporate yet also transcend 'modernity' – are attracting the rich attention they deserve. To give just one example, over a century ago Steiner was the leading international scholar of Goethe's much-neglected scientific works – and yet it is only more recently (cf. Bortoft, 1996; Naydler, 1996) that Goethe's scientific worldview is beginning to gain widespread recognition within the emerging paradigm of 'New Science' championed by authorities like Drs Rupert Sheldrake and Jeremy Naydler in Britain, and Professor Arthur Zajonc and Frijof Capra in the USA.

Just over 100 years after the founding of the first Waldorf school in Stuttgart in September 1919 under Steiner's careful direction, Steiner Waldorf education is today the world's largest and most rapidly growing independent schooling movement in every continent on the planet, with the Waldorf educational approach proving so adaptable to different cultural conditions that it is represented in countries and continents the world over.

Steiner spent the last 15 years of his life lecturing and writing about education, and those of his educational works translated into English number approaching 20 volumes (some of which are listed at the end of this chapter). In this short chapter I can only present the bare bones of his educational approach; the interested reader can start with the 'Further Reading' material listed at the end of this chapter.

Steiner was a relentless scourge of the one-sided materialism that prevailed in his day, and he brought a spiritually informed perspective to his educational worldview, which viewed the human being as far more than just a material body. Steiner's so-called 'four-fold' view of the human being took account of the human being's non-material, subtle 'energy bodies' as well the sense-perceptible material body. Although these 'super-sensible' insights fed directly into and informed his educational philosophy and praxis, it is important to emphasise that one can gain a considerable amount of wisdom and insight from his educational works without necessarily accepting his own spiritual worldview (sometimes called Anthroposophy).

Steiner's educational philosophy is *developmentally informed*, with the teacher's task being to provide the appropriate learning environment consistent with the needs of the unfolding child. This in turn requires, on the teacher's part, a profound understanding of the developing human being; and much of Steiner's educational and other writings are taken up with a detailed articulation of such an understanding. There is a very 'modern' feel to this aspect of Steiner's approach, with the growing child's rhythm of development being broadly organised in seven-year phases which correlate with the unfolding 'bodies' of the developing child (physical, etheric and astral), with the ego being the active principle (or the Self) that works in/through/with the astral, etheric and physical bodies.

Between birth and the age of 7, on Steiner's view the child learns predominantly through imitation, repetition, rhythmical activity and free, unhindered play; and his/her main task is the (unconscious) development of the will in an atmosphere of reverence, along with the healthy development of the physical body. Then, from age 7 to 14, the child lives predominantly in the feeling realm, and learns through living pictures with an emphasis on beauty and artistic creativity. And from age 14 to 21, the child comes into the realm of ideas, thinking, and a deep desire for truth and understanding.

In this schema, quasi-formal learning is strictly avoided until the change of teeth (normally between age 6 and 7), and Steiner emphasised how the introduction of formal, abstract learning (e.g. reading and writing) before this age was positively harmful to the child – a finding which is beginning to be confirmed by recent child-developmental research. This is an issue that will be addressed later in the book.

Between age 7 and 14, the Waldorf pupil ideally has the same Class Teacher for eight years, providing a continuity and intimacy of relationship which is notably missing in the fragmented curriculum of mainstream education, and with this former approach being profoundly nourishing for the growing child. Waldorf-educated alumni typically speak with glowing appreciation when recalling the formative influence of this Class Teacher relationship. (This is a key issue with regard to the traumatising impact on children aged 7–14 of a forced, no-notice school closure, and how it brutalises this deep attachment relationship; again, this issue will be returned to later.)

In the upper school from age 14 onwards, subject teaching predominates, but 'subjects' are taught in a 'trans-disciplinary' way which as far as possible avoids the artificial disciplinary boundaries of conventional education. Thus, science is taught in a living, 'Goethean-observational' way (e.g. Bortoft, 1996; Seamon & Zajonc, 1998) which unites science with an artistic sensibility that is typically missing in conventional science teaching. Despite the comparative lack of competitive testing and examinations in Waldorf education, Waldorf-educated pupils typically obtain public examination results significantly above the national average, and many have highly successful university education and subsequent academic careers.

The holistic approach in Waldorf education means that teaching is always done 'from the whole to the part' (Reinsmith, 1989), and not the other way around – thereby providing an antidote to the mechanistic reductionism of the modernist worldview. Moreover, the more recently articulated holistic notions of 'emotional intelligence' (Daniel Goleman – Goleman, 1996) and 'spiritual intelligence' (Danah Zohar – Zohar & Marshall, 2001) were quite explicitly prefigured by Steiner in his educational philosophy, critical as he was of the one-sided intellectualism which he saw as being only capable of giving a severely limited understanding of the world (cf. Betti, 2019).

A number of other Waldorf pedagogical principles are worth noting. First, Waldorf education is very practical, with as much emphasis being placed on creative craft and manual activity as on intellectual and academic pursuits. For Steiner, the healthy pursuit of the former can only enrich and deepen the latter – holism again.

Next, education is very much seen as a living creative *art* rather than as a science, with *human relationship* being an absolutely central aspect of any educational experience. Relatedly, the *being-qualities* of the teacher are seen as being more important than the amount of purely factual information that the teacher knows; and it follows that the teacher's own *personal development* is seen as being a quite crucial aspect of being a Waldorf teacher. These are just some of the so-called 'intangibles' of effective teaching, which Steiner repeatedly emphasised, and which a mechanistic, positivist approach to teaching either undervalues or, at worst, completely ignores. Education at its best is also seen by Steiner as being an intrinsically *healing force* for the child.

Organisationally, the Waldorf school normally has a 'flat' power structure and 'distributed leadership', with no headmaster/mistress, and with a College of Teachers which works consensually to decide matters of school policy, administration etc. In Steiner's time this was a quite unheard-of social innovation; and it is only in recent years that the emergence of similar organisational forms is beginning to make itself felt within 'new paradigm' organisational arrangements (e.g. Senge, 2006). Freedom is, therefore, a central aspect of this educational approach; and the aim is to enable and empower young people to enter the world as free, independent, creative thinkers, free of the quasi-authoritarian ideology that, almost unnoticed, arguably infects much conventional schooling due to inappropriate political intrusions into the world of education (and of which Steiner himself was highly critical; on the theme of freedom in education from wide-ranging perspectives, see, for example, Carnie et al., 1995; Pring, 1995; and Young, 1995).

Waldorf education has much to contribute to current educational debates. To give just a few examples. In Steiner's development of his 'Threefold Social Order' notion (e.g. Large & Briault, 2018 – see pp. 23–4) that transcends both free-market capitalism and centralised state-socialism, Steiner tirelessly argued against the State having any direct input into the educational sphere – a view that is gaining far wider currency in the light of the rampant ethos of central political control that has engulfed state education in recent decades via 'Audit Culture' values and practices (Power, 1997; Strathern, 2000a, b) – issues that will be returned to in what follows.

Moreover, the 'death of childhood' is a theme that is increasingly echoing throughout modern culture (Postman, 1995; Buckingham, 2000; Palmer, 2015; Creasy & Corby, 2019), and Steiner was a fierce defender of the right to a childhood unburdened by imposed and misguided adult-centric agendas. Finally, it is implicit in Steiner's philosophy that the use of computers and television by young children will often be harmful – and again, modern research findings are increasingly bearing this out, well demonstrated in the writings of mainstream scientist Baroness Susan Greenfield (e.g. Greenfield, 2018–9; see also Brinton & Glöckler, 2019).

Overall, then, Steiner's educational philosophy and Waldorf praxis together provide an impressively coherent and comprehensive 'post-modern', 'new paradigm' antidote to the worst excesses of a materialistic worldview that has arguably brought our world to the foothills of ecological disaster and unsustainability; and in this sense it is supremely relevant as we struggle through the death throes of 'modernity' and towards a new post-materialistic worldview. The intention of Steiner Waldorf education, and of the teachers across the world who choose this schooling paradigm, is to support generations to come in nurturing caring citizens who learn to experience qualities like reverence, respect and gratitude for the world we live in. To this end, Waldorf education deliberately fosters creativity, imagination and a holistic understanding of the world, nurturing and inspiring children's inner potential in becoming sensible, responsible, and 'emotionally and spiritually intelligent' members of society.

I close this orientating chapter with some verbatim education quotations from Rudolf Steiner, which highlight very well the fundamental differences between Waldorf education and the educational model that government is currently intent on imposing on our schooling system.

- It is of great importance to find an answer to the needs of our times through an education which is based on a real understanding of humankind's evolution.

- If… mechanical thinking is carried into education,… there is no longer any natural gift for approaching the child himself. We experiment with the child because we can no longer approach his heart and soul.

- If... the teacher continues to overload [the child's] mind, he will induce certain symptoms of anxiety. And if... he still continues to cram the child with knowledge in the usual way, disturbances in the child's growing forces will manifest themselves. For this reason the teacher should have no hard and fast didactic system.

- For real life, love is the greatest power of knowledge. And without this love it is utterly impossible to attain to a knowledge of man which could form the basis of a true art of education.

- You cannot teach a child to be good merely by explanation... What you actually are... is the most essential thing of all for the child.

- The school must be run in such a way that one does not set up an abstract ideal, but allows the school to develop out of the teachers and out of the pupils.

- Illnesses that appear in later life are often only the result of educational errors made in the very earliest years of childhood. This is why... education... must study the human being as a whole from birth until death.

- (On teacher training): It is always a matter of concern when someone has passed examinations; he can still undoubtedly be an extremely clever person, but this must be in spite of having passed examinations.

- In a State school, everything is strictly defined... everything is planned with exactitude. With us everything depends on the free individuality of each single teacher... Classes are entrusted entirely to the individuality of the class teacher; ...what we seek to achieve must be achieved in the most varied ways. *It is never a question of external regulations.* [italics added]

- A basic principle of... a Threefold Social Order is to work towards an independent school system, making it free of the

State so that the State does not even inspect schools. The activity of self-administered schools should arise purely from cultural needs.

- The important thing is that we do not rob teachers of their strengths of personality by forcing them to work within the confines of government regulations.

- It is inappropriate to work towards standardising human souls through future educational methods or school organisation.

- Our education… only lives when it is carried out. It cannot truly be described, it must be experienced.

- It is sometimes difficult to lay hold of these really imponderable elements that are flowing from the soul of the teacher to that of the child and back again, for they are changing every moment while the teaching and education proceed. We must acquire a vision, a soul vision, to perceive the delicate, fleeting elements that play from soul to soul, and possibly we only come to understand the individual in himself when we are able to understand these intimate, spiritual currents playing between human beings.

- Without entering into [subtle distinctions] one cannot understand what education really is.

- How can a soul be educated if it is first eliminated by materialistic conceptions? This elimination of the soul was characteristic of the materialism… which still prevails widely today in human activity.

- Our function becomes that of an awakener of the child's soul and not a crammer of the soul.

- Any attempts to transform the methods of education must… [bring] it back into the domain of the soul and feelings, and into what wells forth from the whole nature of man.

- The State will tell us how to teach and what results to aim for, and what the State prescribes will be bad. Its targets are the worst ones imaginable, yet it expects to get the best possible results. Today's politics work in the direction of regimentation, and it will go even further than this in its attempts to make people conform. Human beings will be treated like puppets on strings, and this will be treated as progress in the extreme. Institutions like schools will be organised in the most arrogant and unsuitable manner.

Further Reading on Steiner Waldorf Education

Note: There exists an enormous literature on Steiner Waldorf education. In order to make this Further Reading section of manageable length, I have focused exclusively on Steiner's original works, and secondary-source books and academic papers. A more comprehensive bibliography, including book chapters, articles, theses, conference papers and films, can be obtained from the author on request at: https://tinyurl.com/sdmohuo.

Some Key Books on Education by Rudolf Steiner

Note: There exist multiple editions of Steiner's education writings, many with different titles – especially those reproducing his many lecture cycles on education and related themes. The list below is therefore by no means comprehensive, but it does give a clear indication of his formidable *oeuvre* in the education field. For a comprehensive listing of all of Steiner's writings in education, with corresponding volume number from the Complete Works edition (in German the 'Gesamtausgabe', or 'complete edition' abbreviated, 'GA' in German, and 'CW' in English) as assigned by the Rudolf Steiner Archives in Dornach, Switzerland, see https://www.rudolfsteinerweb.com/Rudolf_Steiner_in_English_Search_Results.php.

Steiner, R. (1967). *Discussions with Teachers. Fifteen Discussions and Three Lectures of August to September 1919 in Stuttgart, Germany.* London: Rudolf Steiner Press.

Steiner, R. (1968). *The Essentials of Education: Five Lectures Delivered during the Educational Conference at the Waldorf School, Stuttgart, 8–12 April 1924*, 3rd edn. London: Rudolf Steiner Press.

Steiner, R. (1969). *Education as a Social Problem: Six Lectures, Dornach, 9–17 August 1919.* Hudson, NY: Anthroposophic Press.

Steiner, R. (1972). *A Modern [New] Art of Education: Fourteen Lectures Given in Ilkley, Yorkshire, 5–17 August 1923.* London: Rudolf Steiner Press.

Steiner, R. (1982). *Balance in Teaching. Four Lectures, 15, 16, 21, 22 September 1920*. Spring Valley, NY: Mercury Press.

Steiner, R. (1985). *An Introduction to Waldorf Education*. New York: Anthroposophic Press.

Steiner, R. (1988). *The Child's Changing Consciousness and Waldorf Education*. Hudson, NY: Anthroposophic Press; London: Rudolf Steiner Press.

Steiner, R. (1989). *Conferences with the Teachers of the Waldorf School in Stuttgart, Volume 4, 1923–1924*. Forest Row, East Sussex: Steiner Schools Fellowship Publications.

Steiner, R. (1995). *The Kingdom of Childhood: Introductory Talks on Waldorf Education. Seven Lectures, 12–20 August 1924, Torquay*. New York: Anthroposophic Press.

Steiner, R. (1995). *The Spirit of the Waldorf School: Lectures Surrounding the Founding of the First Waldorf School, Stuttgart, 1919*. Hudson, NY: Anthroposophic Press.

Steiner, R. (1995). *Waldorf Education and Anthroposophy 1. Nine Lectures, 23 February 1921 to 16 September 1922* (various locations). Hudson, NY: Anthroposophic Press.

Steiner, R. (1996). *The Education of the Child in the Light of Spiritual Science: The Education of the Child and Early Lectures on Education*. Gt Barrington, Mass.: Anthroposphic Press.

Steiner, R. (1996). *Rudolf Steiner in the Waldorf School: Lectures and Addresses to Children, Parents, and Teachers, 1919*. Hudson, NY: Anthroposophic Press.

Steiner, R. (1997). *The Roots of Education: Five Lectures Given in Berne, 13–17 April 1924*. Hudson, NY: Anthroposophic Press.

Steiner. R. (1998). *Education for Special Needs: The Curative Education Course: 12 Lectures, 25 June to 7 July 1924, Dornach, Switzerland*, 3rd edn. Forest Row, East Sussex: Rudolf Steiner Press.

Steiner, R. (1998). *Faculty Meetings with Rudolf Steiner, Volume 1, 1919–1922*. New York: Anthroposophic Press.

Steiner, R. (2000). *Practical Advice to Teachers. 14 Lectures of 21 August to 5 September 1919 in Stuttgart, Germany*. Great Barrington, Mass.: Anthroposophic Press.

Steiner, R. (2001). *The Renewal of Education. 14 Lectures, 20 April to 11 May 1920 in Basel, Switzerland*. New York: SteinerBooks.

Steiner, R. (2004). *Human Values in Education. Ten Lectures, 17–24 July 1924, Arnheim, Holland*. Great Barrington, Mass.: Anthroposophic Press.

Steiner, R. (2004). *The Spiritual Ground of Education. Nine Lectures, 16–25 August 1922, Oxford*. Great Barrington, Mass.: Anthroposophic Press.

Books on Steiner Waldorf Education

Allanson, A. & Teensma, N. (2018). *Writing to Reading the Steiner Waldorf Way: Foundations of Creative Literacy in Classes 1 and 2*. Stroud, Gloucestershire: Hawthorn Press.

Avison, K. (2016). *A Handbook for Steiner-Waldorf Class Teachers,* 3rd edn. Edinburgh: Floris Books.

Britz-Creclius, H. (1996). *Children at Play: Using Waldorf Principles to Foster Childhood Development*. Rochester, VT: Inner Traditions.

Byers, P., Dillard, C., Easton, F., Henry, M., McDermott, R., Oberman I., & Uhrmacher, P.B. (1996). *Waldorf Education in an Inner-City Public School: The Urban Waldorf School of Milwaukee*. Spring Valley, NY: Parker Courtney Press (for the Waldorf Education Research Institute of North America).

Carlgren, F. (2008). *Education towards Freedom: Rudolf Steiner Education – A Survey of the Work of Waldorf Schools throughout the World*, 3rd edn. Edinburgh: Floris Books.

Childs, G. (1992). *Steiner Education in Theory and Practice: A Guide to Rudolf Steiner's Educational Principles*. Edinburgh: Floris Books.

Childs, G. (1999). *Truth, Beauty and Goodness: Steiner-Waldorf Education as a Demand of Our Time*. London: Temple Lodge.

Clouder, C. (ed.) (2003). *Rudolf Steiner Education: An Introductory Reader*. Forest Row, Sussex: Rudolf Steiner Press.

Clouder, C. & Rawson, M. (1998). *Waldorf Education* (Rudolf Steiner's Ideas in Practice). Edinburgh: Floris Books.

Edmunds, L.F. (1987). *Rudolf Steiner Education: The Waldorf School*, 2nd edn. London: Pharos.

Edmunds, F. (2004). *An Introduction to Steiner Education: The Waldorf School*, revised edn. London: Rudolf Steiner Press / Sofia Books.

Finser, T. (1994). *School as a Journey: The Eight Year Odyssey of a Waldorf Teacher and His Class*. Great Barrington, Mass.: Anthroposophic Press.

Finser, T. (1995). *Research: Reflections and Suggestions for Teachers for Creating a Community of Research in Waldorf Schools*. Fair Oaks, Calif.: Association of Waldorf Schools of North America.

Gladstone, F. (ed.) (1997). *Republican Academies*. Forest Row: Steiner Schools Fellowship Publications.

Goral, M. (2009). *Transformational Teaching: Waldorf-inspired Methods in the Public School*. Forest Row: Rudolf Steiner Press; and Great Barrington, Mass.: SteinerBooks.

Grunelius E.M. (1991/1966). *Early Childhood Education and the Waldorf School Plan*. STP Books.

Harwood, A.C. (1940). *The Way of a Child*. London: Rudolf Steiner Press.

Harwood, A.C. (1958). *The Recovery of Man in Childhood: A Study in the Educational Work of Rudolph Steiner*. London: Hodder and Stoughton.

Hofrichter, H. (2002). *Waldorf: The Story behind the Name*, extended edn. Stuttgart: Pädagogischen Forschungsstelle beim Bund der Freien Waldorfschulen.

Jaffke, F. (1996). *Work and Play in Early Childhood*. Edinburgh: Floris Books.

Jaffke, F. (ed.) (2004). *On the Play of the Child: Indications by Rudolf Steiner for Working with Young Children*. Spring Valley, NY: Waldorf Early Childhood Association of North America, on behalf of the International Association of Waldorf Kindergartens.

Kellman, J., Schmitt-Stegman A., & Staley, B. (1996). *Examining the Waldorf Curriculum from an American Viewpoint*. Ann Arbor, Mich.: Pedagogical Section of the Anthroposophical Society in America.

Kiersch, J. (1997). *Foreign Language Teaching in Steiner Waldorf Schools*. Forest Row, Sussex: Steiner Schools Fellowship Publications.

Lamb, G. (2004). *The Social Mission of Waldorf Education*. Fair Oaks, Calif.: Association of Waldorf Schools of North America.

Lissau, M. (2004). *Awakening Intelligence: The Task of the Teacher and the Key Picture of the Learning Process*. Fair Oaks, Calif.: Association of Waldorf Schools of North America.

Male, D. (2006). *The Parent and Child Group Handbook: A Steiner / Waldorf Approach.* Stroud, Gloucestershire: Hawthorn Press.

Masters, B. (2005). *Adventures in Steiner Education: An Introduction to the Waldorf Approach.* London: Rudolf Steiner Press.

Masters, B. (2007). *Steiner Educational and Social Issues: How Waldorf Schooling Addresses the Problems of Society.* London: Rudolf Steiner Press.

Masters, B. (2018). *Grammar Teaching: Why, What, When, How.* Stourbridge: Wynstones Press.

Mitchell, D. (2006). *Windows into Waldorf: An Introduction to Waldorf Education.* Fair Oaks, Calif.: Association of Waldorf Schools of North America.

Mattke, H.-J. (ed.) (1994). *Waldorf Education World-Wide: Celebrating the 75th Anniversary of the Uhlandshöhe Waldorf School in Stuttgart.* Stuttgart: Freie Waldorfschule Uhlandshöhe.

Mazzone, A. & Laing, S. (2017). *A Passionate Schooling: Key Ideas behind Steiner Waldorf Education.* lulu.com.

Mitchell, D. & Gerwin, D. (2007). *Survey of Waldorf Graduates. Phase II.* Wilton, NH: Research Institute for Waldorf Education.

Mitchell, D. & Livingston, P. (ed.) (1999). *Will-developed Intelligence: Handwork and Practical Arts in the Waldorf School.* Fair Oaks, Calif.: Association of Waldorf Schools of North America.

Müller, H. (1983). *Healing Forces in the Word and its Rhythms.* Forest Row, Sussex: Rudolf Steiner Schools Fellowship Publications.

Murphy, C. (1991). *Emil Molt and the Beginnings of the Waldorf School Movement: Sketches from an Autobiography.* Edinburgh: Floris Books.

Nicol, J. (2016). *Bringing the Steiner Waldorf Approach to Your Early Years Practice,* 2nd edn. Abingdon, Oxon: Routledge.

Nicol, J. & Taplin, J. (2012). *Understanding the Steiner Waldorf Approach: Early Years Education in Practice.* London: Routledge.

Nobel, A. (1991). *Educating through Art: The Steiner Waldorf Approach.* Edinburgh: Floris Books.

Oberski, I. (2005). *Learning to Think in Steiner-Waldorf Schools.* University of Stirling, Institute of Education: IACEP, July; available at https://tinyurl.com/vx5xs4q (accessed 9 March 2020).

Ogletree, E.J. (1998). *International Survey of the Status of Waldorf.* University of Illinois.

Oldfield, L. (2003). *Free to Learn: Introducing Steiner Waldorf Early Childhood Education.* Stroud, Gloucestershire: Hawthorn Press; 2nd edn, 2012.

Parker-Rees, R. (ed.) (2011). *Meeting the Child in Steiner Kindergartens: An Exploration of Beliefs, Values and Practices.* London: Routledge.

Petrash, J. (2000). *Understanding Waldorf Education: Teaching from the Inside Out.* Beltsville, MD: Gryphon Press; Edinburgh: Floris (2002).

Piening, E. & Lyons, N. (eds) (1979). *Educating as an Art: Essays on the Rudolf Steiner Method – Waldorf Education.* New York: Rudolf Steiner School Press.

Querido, R. (1995). *Creativity in Education: The Waldorf Approach.* Fair Oaks, Calif.: Rudolf Steiner College Press.

Rawson, M. & Masters, B. (eds) (1997). *Towards Creative Teaching: Working with the Curriculum of Classes 1–8 in Steiner Waldorf Schools.* Forest Row, Sussex: Steiner Schools Fellowship Publications.

Rawson, M. & Rose, M. (2006). *Ready to Learn: From Birth to School Readiness.* Stroud, Gloucestershire: Hawthorn Press.

Richards, M.C. (1981). *Toward Wholeness: Rudolf Steiner Education in America.* Middletown, Conn.: Wesleyan University Press.

Rist, G. & Schneider, P. (1979). *Integrating Vocational and General Education: A Rudolf Steiner School. Case Study of the Hibernia School, Herne, Federal Republic of Germany.* Education Resources Information Center.

Sagarin, S.K. (2011). *The Story of Waldorf Education in the United States.* Great Barrington, Mass.: Steiner Books.

Schubert, E. (1999). *Teaching Mathematics for First and Second Grades in Waldorf Schools.* Fair Oaks, Calif.: Rudolf Steiner College Press.

Schwartz, E. (1999). *Millennial Child: Transforming Education in the Twenty-first Century*. Great Barrington, Mass.: Anthroposophic Press.

Schweitzer, S. (2006). *Well I Wonder: Childhood in the Modern World*. Forest Row, Sussex: Rudolf Steiner Press.

Spock, M. (1985). *Teaching as a Lively Art*. Spring Valley, NY: Anthroposophic Press.

Stehlik, T. (2003). *Each Parent Carries the Flame: Waldorf Schools as Sites for Promoting Lifelong Learning, Creating Community and Educating for Social Renewal*. Flaxton, Queensland: Postpressed.

Stockmeyer, K. (1969). *Rudolf Steiner's Curriculum for Waldorf Schools*. Forest Row, East Sussex: Rudolf Steiner Press.

von Baravalle, H. (1967). *The International Waldorf School Movement*. Spring Valley, NY: St George Publications.

von Heydebrand, C. (ed.) (1986). *The Curriculum of the First Waldorf School*. Forest Row, Sussex: Steiner Schools Fellowship Publications.

Wilkinson, R. (2005). *The Temperaments in Education*. Fair Oaks, Calif.: Rudolf Steiner College Press.

Willby, M.E. (ed.) (2005). *Learning Difficulties: A Guide for Teachers, Waldorf Insights and Practical Approaches*, 2nd edn. Fair Oaks, Calif.: Rudolf Steiner College Press.

Woods, P., Ashley, M. & Woods, G. (2005). *Steiner Schools in England*, Research Report 645. London: Department for Education and Skills; Centre for Research in Education and Democracy, Faculty of Education, University of the West of England, available at: https://tinyurl.com/rchq6dp (accessed 8 March 2020).

Woods, P.A. & Woods, G.J. (2006). *Feedback Report (Michael Hall Steiner School): Collegial Leadership in Action*. Aberdeen: University of Aberdeen.

Academic Papers on Steiner Waldorf Education

Ashley, M. (2008). Here's what you must think about nuclear power: grappling with the spiritual ground of children's judgement inside and outside Steiner Waldorf education. *International Journal of Children's Spirituality*, 13 (1): 65–74.

Astley, K. & Jackson, P. (2000). Doubts on spirituality: interpreting Waldorf ritual. *International Journal of Educational Research*, 5, (2): 221–7; available at https://tinyurl.com/vsqhbhs (accessed 12 March 2020).

Barnes, H. (1980). An introduction to Waldorf education. *Teachers College Record*, 81 (3): 322–36.

Cox, M.V. & Rolands, A. (2000). The effect of three different educational approaches on children's drawing ability: Steiner, Montessori and traditional. *British Journal of Educational Psychology*, 70: 485–503.

Dahlin, B. (2009). On the path towards thinking: learning from Martin Heidegger and Rudolf Steiner. *Studies in the Philosophy of Education*, 28: 537–54.

Dahlin, B. (2010). A state-independent education for citizenship? Comparing beliefs and values related to civic and moral issues among students in Swedish mainstream and Steiner Waldorf schools. *Journal of Beliefs and Values*, 31 (2): 165–80.

Dhondt, P., van der Vijver, N. & Verstraete, P. (2015). The possibility of an unbiased history of Steiner/Waldorf education? *Contemporary European History*, 24 (4): 639–49.

Easton, F. (1997). Educating the whole child, 'head, heart and hands': learning from the Waldorf experience. *Theory into Practice*, 36 (2): 87–95.

Ensign, J. (1996). A conversation between John Dewey and Rudolf Steiner: a comparison of Waldorf and progressive education. *Educational Theory*, 46 (2): 175–88; available at https://tinyurl.com/s6lfsaz (accessed 12 March 2020).

Gardner, M.E. (1992). School rituals as educational contexts: symbolizing the world, others, and self in Waldorf and college prep schools. *International Journal of Qualitative Studies in Education*, 5(4): 295–309; available at https://tinyurl.com/u4qdpvt (accessed 12 March 2020).

Gidley, J.M. (2007). Educational imperatives of the evolution of consciousness: the integral visions of Rudolf Steiner and Ken Wilber. *International Journal of Children's Spirituality*, 12 (2): 117–35.

Ginsberg, I. (1982). Jean Piaget and Rudolf Steiner: stages of child development and implications for pedagogy. *Teachers College Record*, 84 (Winter): 327–37.

Grant, M. (1999). Steiner and the humours: the survival of Ancient Greek science. *British Journal of Educational Studies*, 47 (1): 56–70.

Hallam, J., Egan, S., & Kirkham, J. A. (2016). An investigation into the ways in which art is taught in an English Waldorf Steiner school. *Thinking Skills and Creativity*, 19:136–45.

Henry, M.E. (1992). School rituals as educational contexts: symbolizing the world, others, and self in Waldorf and college pre schools. *International Journal of Qualitative Studies in Education*, 5 (4): 295–309.

Hutchingson, R. & Hutchingson, J. (1993). Waldorf education as a program for gifted students. *Journal for the Education of the Gifted*, 16 (4): 400–19; available at https://tinyurl.com/v5regyx (accessed 10 March 2020).

Lim, B. (2004). Aesthetic discourses in early childhood settings: Dewey, Steiner, and Vygotsky. *Early Child Development and Care*, 174 (5): 473–86.

McDermott, R., Byers, P., Dillard, C., Easton, F., Henry, M., & Uhrmacher, P. B. (1996). Waldorf education in an inner-city public school. *Urban Review*, 28 (2): 119–40.

Nicholson, D.W. (2000). Layers of experience: forms of representation in a Waldorf school classroom. *Journal of Curriculum Studies*, 32 (4): 575–87.

Nielsen, T.W. (2006). Towards a pedagogy of imagination: a phenomenological case study of holistic education. *Ethnography and Education*, 1 (2): 247–64.

Nielsen, T. (2007). Tracing the origin of Rudolf Steiner's pedagogy of imagination. *History of Education Review*, 36 (1): 49–60.

Oberski, I. (2006). Learning to think in Steiner-Waldorf schools. *Journal of Cognitive Education and Psychology*, 5 (3): 336–49.

Oberski, I. (2007). Validating a Steiner-Waldorf teacher education programme. *Journal of Teaching in Higher Education*, 12 (1): 135–9.

Oberski, I.M. (2009). Fostering curriculum for excellence: teachers' freedom and creativity through developing their intuition and imagination: some insights from Steiner-Waldorf education. *Scottish Educational Review*, 41 (2): 20–31.

Oberski, I. (2011). Rudolf Steiner's philosophy of freedom as a basis for spiritual education? *International Journal of Children's Spirituality*, 16 (1): 5–17.

O'Connor, D. & Angus, J. (2014). Give them time – an analysis of school readiness in early education system: a Steiner Waldorf perspective. *Education 3–13: International Journal of Primary, Elementary and Early Years Education*, 42 (5): 488–97.

Ogletree, E.J. (1974). Rudolf Steiner: unknown educator. *Elementary School Journal*, 74 (6): 344–51.

Ogletree, E.J. (1975). Geometric form drawing: a perceptual-motor approach to preventive remediation (the Steiner approach). *Journal of Special Education*, 9 (3): 237–45.

Ogletree, E.J. (1976). Eurythmy: a therapeutic art of movement. *Journal of Special Education*, 10 (3): 305–19.

Ogletree, E.J. (1987). Eurythmy: art of movement in the Waldorf schools. *Journal of the Society for Accelerative Learning and Teaching*, 12 (1–4): 65–84.

O'Shiel, P. & O'Flynn, S. (1998). Education as an art: an appraisal of Waldorf education. *Irish Educational Studies*, 17 (1): 337–52.

Paull, J. (2011). Rudolf Steiner and the Oxford Conference: the birth of Waldorf education in Britain. *European Journal of Educational Studies*, 3 (1): 53–66.

Paull, J. & Hennig, B. (2020). Rudolf Steiner education and Waldorf schools: centenary world maps of the global diffusion of 'The School of the Future'. *Journal of Social Sciences and Humanities*, 6 (1): 24–33.

Reinsmith, W.A. (1989). The whole in every part: Steiner and Waldorf schooling.

Educational Forum, 54 (1): 79–91.

Rivers, I. & Soutter, A. (1996). Bullying and the Steiner school ethos. *School Psychology International,* 17: 359–77.

Sobo, E.J. (2014). Play's relation to health and well-being in preschool and kindergarten: a Waldorf (Steiner) education perspective. *International Journal of Play,* 3 (1): 9–23.

Sobo, E.J. (2015). Salutogenic education? Movement and whole child health in a Waldorf (Steiner) school. *Medical Anthropology Quarterly,* 29 (2): 137–56.

Uhrmacher, P.B. (1993). Coming to know the world through Waldorf education. *Journal of Curriculum and Supervision,* 9 (1): 87–104.

Uhrmacher, P.B. (1995). Uncommon schooling: a historical look at Rudolf Steiner, Anthroposophy, and Waldorf education. *Curriculum Inquiry,* 25 (4): 381–406.

Ullrich, H. (1994). Rudolf Steiner (1861–1925). *Prospects: Quarterly Review of Comparative Education,* 24 (3–4): 555–72.

Woods G., O'Neill, M., & Woods, P. A. (1997). Spiritual values in education: lessons from Steiner? *International Journal of Children's Spirituality,* 2 (2): 25–40.

.

.

PART II

Deconstructing the Wynstones Ofsted Closure Report

CHAPTER 2

The Question of Safeguarding

Risk is not unambiguous… Many social issues
are not black or white.
ROB CREASY

Can we know the risks we face, now or in the future? No, we cannot: but yes,
we must act as if we do.
M. DOUGLAS & A. WILDAVSKY, quoted by MICHAEL POWER

Introduction

Safeguarding is an exceedingly complex question, as well as being a cultural preoccupation which is historically situated, with the conscious and unconscious drivers underpinning it needing to be thought about with the care and subtlety that such a complex issue requires. I say 'historically situated' here because as Creasy (2020, p. 49) points out, the notion of 'risk' is not some universally transcendent datum of human experience, but rather, 'risk is very often socially constructed, especially in terms of how we respond to what we perceive as risky'.

It is also important to pose the wider question as to why there is such a heavy emphasis on risk and safeguarding in England compared with many other countries around the world – a question that is unfortunately beyond the scope of this short book. Suffice to quote Page (2017) at this juncture in an observation of great relevance to this book, when he writes that 'risk has become central to the management of the contemporary school and is *the prime antecedent of the massive increase in the surveillance of teachers'* (p. 1001, my italics)

This chapter forms the core of this counter-report, as safeguar,ding was cited by the Department for Education as the key reason why Wynstones School was forced to close; and there are copious criticisms on safeguarding-related issues in Ofsted's inspection report which need a detailed response and careful rebuttal.

Parton (2010, p. 593) points out that 'safeguarding' is a word used in England (and to a lesser extent in Wales), being 'a very fluid idea, full of considerable confusion', with its roots in child protection deriving from debates in the 1990s around the abuse of children in residential care. And similarly, Power (2004, pp. 13–14) maintains that the notion of risk 'remains elusive, contested and inherently controversial' – with this very ambiguity paradoxically being 'a necessary feature of its widespread impact' (p. 14).

The term 'safeguarding' was first defined in 2006 in *Working Together* (HM Government, 2006, quoted in ibid.). According to Parton, the inquiry into the death of Victoria Climbié was used as a vehicle for introducing wholesale changes in children's services; and crucially, 'it was only ever very partially concerned with child abuse' (Parton, 2010, p. 593). This in turn has generated confusion in policy and practice at both central government and local level, Parton argues; and 'there remains ambiguity about what safeguarding means and what its key focus and rationale is [sic]' (ibid.) And more presciently still, 'These are complicated issues and have major implications for all concerned... – including OFSTED' (p. 593). So with the notion of safeguarding being replete with tensions and confusions, there is a 'need to consider "the big picture" when it comes to policy in relation to children and their families' (p. 594) – something that I will certainly be endeavouring to do in this chapter.

Moreover, if policy-making around this difficult issue is being, at least in part, driven by an unprocessed 'culture of fear' and low-trust paranoia (as I will argue below), then there are very grave implications indeed for the possible wrong-headedness of much policy-making in this field. More specifically, the uncritical inserting of safeguarding concerns into an approach that demands rule-bound Audit Culture *proceduralism*' has considerable dangers ('meaning 'an approach that narrowly sticks to fixed procedure, whatever the unique contextual circumstances') – especially if there is no space within the procedures for exercising nuanced professional judgement in what are always unavoidably multi-layered and uniquely complex circumstances, and into which those working on the inside of the system will have considerably more insight and understanding than those viewing the system from the outside on a one-off basis.

Safeguarding is an issue which necessarily takes a prominent place in this counter-report, as concerns over safeguarding constituted the pretext for closing Wynstones School. Below I will subject the published Ofsted criticisms around safeguarding to forensic analysis, as well as offering a wider, contextualising perspective on the safeguarding phenomenon as a relatively recent cultural preoccupation in England. The latter is essential in order to place Ofsted's judgements in a wider context, as there is a considerable and convincing critical/academic literature which challenges modern cultural preoccupations (and, some say, obsessions) with safeguarding. If it can be shown – which I believe it can – that couching safeguarding concerns within an inflexible rule-bound proceduralism is not only grossly inadequate and inappropriate, but actually risks committing major abuses *on its own account* by virtue of the system's inflexible implementation, then severe doubts will inevitably be cast on the appropriateness of judgements and assessments made that are solely informed by that rule-bound proceduralism – and which have massive impacts on the welfare of the people inhabiting the system that is being policed.

This chapter therefore has a dual purpose: first, to open up the issue of safeguarding as a recent cultural phenomenon to critical scrutiny; and then within this context, to question the way in which Ofsted has perceived and represented safeguarding issues in its school inspection report, with the Department for Education then deploying Ofsted's problematic contentions as the pretext for closing a school virtually overnight.

Safeguarding – It's Complex, and Problematic...

I begin this section with a telling anecdote. When I worked as a professional psychotherapist back in the 2000s, on several occasions I worked with clients whose families had been destroyed as a direct result of unsubstantiated allegations of child abuse. Specifically, these families had been reported to Social Services as a matter of procedure around concerns about suspected child abuse – leading to subsequent detailed investigations of the family. But even though the families were subsequently given a completely clean bill of health and the accusations found to be unfounded, the enormous stress and anxiety generated by the investigations let to these families splitting up and the family unit being lost.

Understandably, my clients were outraged by what had happened to their families – and who can blame them? This resonates with what Devine (2018, p, 2) has recently written; viz. 'once a family is referred they may find themselves escalated into a process which requires social workers to assess whether a family may need services within *an inflexible framework designed to deal with cases of significant harm*' (my italics). Under the current safeguarding legislation, 'the vast majority of cases that are referred to local authorities are not cases where systematic and deliberate abuse is found to be occurring' (ibid.); and yet 'the surveillance / policing process is constructed in such a way so as to make it very difficult for a family to extract itself' (ibid., p. 4).

In similar vein, according to Wrennall (2010, p. 309), 'there is extensive evidence of harm to families resulting from Child Protection interventions. Families who have been through Child Protection "assessments" are left traumatized, bewildered, betrayed and powerless.' Cooper et al. (2003, p. 18) also maintain that 'children and families drawn into the child protection process frequently find the whole experience traumatic, and sometimes more traumatic than the abuse itself', with 'children's lives [being] devastated when child removal is substituted for family support' (Wrennall, op. cit.; cf. Carey, 2008). And for Devine (2018), 'Assessment does not only investigate the reason for the referral, but assesses every aspect of a family's private life.... [T]he rise of policing and surveillance ideology has not triggered appropriate safeguards and protections for families caught within its net' (p. 198). Devine goes on to refer to 'an unprecedented level of State paternalism and surveillance of families....', concluding that 'The claim that this rise in State powers and erosion of private rights is justified... is weak.... State power is excessive and not adequately balanced with private rights' (p. 199).

More generally, Wrennall (2010, p. 311) notes the ever-growing sentiment in academia that Anglophone child protection 'has become obsessed with reporting, investigating and monitoring', rather than providing valuable services to the clients in need. Wrennall defines the 'The Trojan Horse theory of Child Protection' to explain 'how a discourse that espouses benevolent, even emancipatory rhetoric, has been complicit in the enactment of social harm against children and their families while simultaneously furthering the economic, commercial and political interests in dataveillance' (p. 318). She maintains further that 'Protection provides a rhetoric that disguises surveillance and disarms opposition, because a justifiable and apparently benign pretext has been found in the ostensible and entirely laudable, aim of protecting children' (p. 304) – presenting widespread evidence of how the pretext of child protection has been used to extend surveillance and disarm citizens.

Developing issues discussed in considerable legal detail in Devine (2018), Wrennall shows how child protection has been structured by the information-sharing model (or so-called 'dataveillance' – p. 305) introduced under New Labour via the 2004 Children Act, to benefit the sectional interests in surveillance, and the negative consequences that this has for children – and with the discourse of child protection being only loosely targeted on preventing child abuse and rehabilitating errant families, but rather, furthering agendas that are contrary to the interests of children and other citizens. For Wrennall, the 2004 Act purveyed 'mystified processes conceal[ing] strategies of power by providing a noble cover story that disarms the usual defences that populations have developed to protect their liberties, dissentions and colourful diverse lifestyles against state intervention' (p. 306).

In blunt terms, for Wrennall 'Child Protection is expanding surveillance and dismantling basic Human and Civil Rights' (ibid.); and it 'creates a rationale for imposing surveillance, invading intimate space, restricting freedoms and appropriating wealth, in the claim that the problem of harm to children is being addressed' (ibid.). Indeed, she goes as far as to claim that 'Presenting surveillance as Child Protection is an example of [Orwellian] "Newspeak"…'(p. 315).

More recently and on similar lines, writing about what Clarke-Wellsmore terms 'the totalitarian overreach of child protection surveillance', we read that 'With no clear boundaries as to what constitutes a legitimate reason for investigation or surveillance, it is quite easy for a family to be wrongly subjected to totalitarian overreach and abuse from the system' (Clarke-Wellsmore (2017, online). For Clarke-Wellsmore, the growing academic literature outlining the devastating effects of current child protection approaches is disturbing, for 'the assessment and investigation process can be equally traumatic for both family and child', with some studies even finding that the whole process is so destructive that even a high portion of abused children report regretting ever disclosing the abuse (ibid.; cf. Wrennall, 2010). And at worst, 'Child Protection rhetoric acts as a trojan horse which enables the state to encroach on the rights of vulnerable populations' (ibid.).

According to Wrennall (2010) and Clarke-Wellsmore (2017), then, in the UK the murder of Victoria Climbié was used as a 'Trojan Horse' to implement an unpopular database, ContactPoint, to cover all British children. And although ContactPoint was scrapped by the new Coalition government in August 2010 after facing accusations of human rights violations, Devine (2018, p. 68) points out that, 'the populating databases remain. The basic position has not therefore changed'. Little wonder, then, that Devine refers to 'the adverse consequences of England's approach [to safeguarding]' (2018, p. 2); and that as a result, school teachers, knowing the unforgiving nature of this 'surveillance / policing process', might understandably be very reluctant to report families they know into a system that will possibly chew them up and generate enormous stress and anxiety, whether there is a genuine safeguarding issue in that family or not.

I raise these questions here because they have direct relevance when considering how professionals responsible for children are positioned by such a system (sometimes 'impossibly', as I will show) – and are then judged, and perhaps condemned, by State agencies that are determined to enforce *the letter* of that safeguarding system without any sensitivity to either its negative unintended consequences, or to professional responsibility and cognitive dissonances. Some of the arguably 'adverse consequences' of this English safeguarding system, and the impossible position of professional dissonance into which it inserts teachers, will become clear in what follows. I believe that the professional anecdote with which I started this section is very relevant to what has happened to Wynstones School around the issue of safeguarding, and the judgements that Ofsted has made of the school around this issue – as will become clear below.

In situations where proceduralism and 'the rule-book' have to be inflexibly followed, this can put dedicated professionals in an impossible, 'damned if you do, damned if you don't' situation. Take the case of a teacher who has concerns about a safeguarding issue in a school family. She may have a strong sense that in the unique circumstances prevailing, and knowing the child and the parents as she does, the best and most appropriate approach would be to speak with the parents first – rather than following a written procedure that demands she immediately reports the case to Social Services. Yet this latter course of action risks a massive breach of trust with the family – perhaps with a family leaving the school as a result (a major issue for a non-State school – and I know of one case when this did happen at Wynstones School) – and at worst, a family unit being wrecked, as described in my psychotherapeutic anecdote at the start of this chapter.

But when the rules say that if a teacher has any concerns they have to report them to the authorities, then *not* to do so risks the condemnation of Ofsted, and very likely, grave repercussions for the school in which they work. *This surely places teachers in a quite impossible position of potentially irreconcilable 'professional cognitive dissonance'*, with their professionalism being hopelessly compromised.

There are also crucial child-development questions involved in all this. As Creasy has shown in his recently published book (Creasy, 2020), the whole question of resilience, risk and safeguarding is a highly complex one. For Creasy, 'experiencing some form of adversity is a crucial part of developing resilience'; 'risk is an essential part of growing up'; 'a fear of children coming to harm means that we prevent them from encountering anything that might be considered risky'; and 'the growing concern with risk… is counterproductive with respect to developing and maintaining resilience' (Creasy, 2020, pp. 8, 16 and 34). Burchell (2020, p. 1) puts it even more starkly: 'not only does safeguarding fail to achieve its stated aims, but… it actively disempowers both those doing the protecting, and those who are seen as needing protection'. And for Wrennall (2010, p. 311), 'disempowerment is ideologically constructed as being in the interests of the disempowered'.

Creasy and Corby (2019) have also recently argued that there is a link – presumably a causal one – between recent reports of increasing levels of unhappiness and mental health problems amongst children, and changes within childhood which restrict and reduce opportunities for children to develop and maintain resilience. On this view, what they call this 'taming of childhood' leads to impoverished childhood experience that fails to provide the space that children need to grow and develop healthily. It could well be, then, that the safeguarding regime currently in place is having a net negative impact on children's wider well-being, resilience and self-esteem – and sensitive, experienced teachers will doubtless be aware of this.

Creasy and Corby also see this taming of childhood and its adverse impact on children's resilience as *a form of violence* against children; they write of

> …an argument in which the cumulative effects of actions which impact upon children or which shape childhood operate as a form of violence against children. This is because actions which serve to tame childhood deny children the opportunities which are necessary for the development and maintenance of resilience, and we see resilience as necessary to enable both a fulfilled childhood and a functioning adulthood. Furthermore, this form of violence denies children their rights to agency. In this respect, it undermines their position as beings. (Creasy & Corby, 2019, p. 126)

And later along the same lines,

> We argue for a recognition that childhood requires freedom if we are to ensure that children are to develop into well-rounded adults. This freedom may be accompanied, however, by some degree of risk. However, if we want children to develop resilience and self-determination, we will not help them by restricting what they can do and attempting to remove all risk from their lives. (p. 127)

And more specifically in relation to the National Curriculum and the Audit Culture (a core concern of this book):

> [S]chools pose a particularly frustrating example in that, although their primary purpose is to provide an education for children, there are many ways in which they act to tame childhood in an attempt to provide *an education which has become increasingly restricted by the National Curriculum*…. [T]he power of schools comes to bear on children for the purpose of establishing a particular representation of the school rather than a concern for each child…. [T]his has been driven by government concerns….. As children become data points, so they are denied a sense of self…. [I]n practice, [viewing children as data points] is what happens…. [Governments] may not have the foresight to understand the impact policies will have on children's lives (pp. 129–30, my italics)

In sum, then, to overprotect children from the experience of risk is to harm the child's capacity to healthily develop resilience – something that Steiner Waldorf pedagogy explicitly recognises, and upon which it endeavours to reach a proportionate view that strikes an empowering balance between the need for safety on the one hand, and the need for challenge and necessary risk on the other. Steiner Waldorf pedagogy would emphatically agree with Creasy (2020, p. 50) when he writes that 'children's lives have been subject to increasing control… and this has seen children having much less freedom than in previous generations'.

Where the line is drawn between good-enough safety and freedom also necessarily then becomes one of professional judgement rather than narrowly rule-bound proceduralism. For in such a complex, paradoxical world, written rules and protocols are simply incapable of doing the subtle job that needs to be done. Yet as Turnbull and Spence have argued (quoted in Creasy, 2020, p. 19), '"risk" has underpinned UK government policy across the field of children and young people since 1996/97' – with 'the state [having] entered more fully into the lives of children and families through limitless government regulations…. [and with] OFSTED appear[ing] open to political interference by government regularly changing the framework for inspectors to suit the latest priority' (Arthur, 2015, p. 311). Creasy also identifies this shift as being from one in which some children are deemed to be at risk, to one in which all children are at risk, and so safeguarding becomes everyone's responsibility (Creasy, 2020, p. 54).

It also follows that the price that is paid for choosing, in an informed way, not to over-control children's worlds, but rather, to place faith in professional judgement and thoughtfulness, is that accidents will occasionally happen, and even 'mistakes' will be made that lead to suffering. Creasy and Corby again:

> [We need to] accept that accidents do happen. Children need to extend themselves and sometimes this will result in a grazed a knee or a cut finger. When children's physical activities are curtailed or when they are restricted in their activities because of concerns about safety, this can be seen as restricting their development. (2019, p. 133)

The price that is paid by everyone by an approach that does everything possible to make sure children are safe is arguably far greater, and more damaging, than is the price of the occasional accident and mistake in a less over-controlled environment. And rather than seeing accidents and mistakes as occurrences that shouldn't have happened, and wouldn't have happened if only one's procedures had been better and more all-embracing, they are an aspect of the experienced life-world, and an unavoidable aspect of a world in which an appropriate and healthily empowering relationship with risk and resilience-building is built and embraced.

This is a key difference between a Steiner Waldorf approach (and indeed many other approaches to child development) and that of Ofsted. To justify its own approach, Ofsted would have to measure and quantify (using appropriate indicators) the quality of the total environment in a Waldorf school as compared with one in a mainstream, Ofsted-regulated one, and demonstrate that the latter were better for children as a whole than the former. According to Rivers and Soutter (1996), there is in fact compelling evidence that the ethos of a school directly impacts the level of bullying. Thus, in researching into three classes of 30 pupils in one Steiner school in the South of England, Rivers and Soutter found a very low level of bullying, despite the fact that many pupils came to the school because they had been victimised elsewhere. At worst, then, the Ofsted approach may well be sacrificing the quality of *the total school environment* through its procedural preoccupation with 'making all children safe' (as the jargon goes).

I know of a number of families, including the Wynstones children themselves, who were horrified and nonplussed when a big fence was erected around the school, presumably at the behest of Ofsted. Anecdotally, one parent has told me that her family chose Wynstones for her children *precisely because* it was a 'high trust' environment; and the erection of a fence around the school felt like a massive compromising of the high-trust school that she wanted and chose for her children. This touches in turn on the question of contrasting and even *incommensurable educational and schooling paradigms*, and the appropriateness of one distinctive paradigm being judged and assessed according to protocols that are singularly unfitting for assessing a school within that paradigm. I will have cause to return to this issue throughout this book, as it constitutes one of the key objections to the way in which Ofsted has assessed and condemned Wynstones School. There are also wider questions here, beyond the scope of this book, as to whether alternative approaches like Steiner Waldorf might be being 'silenced' precisely because they pose such a threat to the ideology that informs Ofsted's and the DfE's Audit Culture proceduralism.

Finally, I maintain that a *culture of fear* (Furedi, 1997) and a managerialist Audit Culture (Power, 1997) constitute a truly toxic cocktail that generates dysfunctionality at every level – from the inspection process to professional integrity, and everything in between. Power (2004, pp. 14–15) characterises the problems plaguing teaching professionals caught up in this system in stark terms:

> [T]he experts who are being made increasingly accountable for what they do are now becoming more preoccupied with managing their own risks. Specifically, *secondary risks to their reputation are becoming as significant as the primary risks for which experts have knowledge and training. This trend is resulting in a dangerous flight from judgement and a culture of defensiveness* that create their own risks for organisations in preparing for, and responding to, a future they cannot know… – driving… professionals to focus more on their personal, legal and reputational risks, rather than on the primary risks embodied in their formal mission. (my italics)

In terms of teachers and their practice, what Power is describing here is a situation in which teaching professionals become more preoccupied with, and worried about, those judging their professionalism (i.e. Ofsted) in the realm of risk and safeguarding than they are about the actual well-being of the 'clients' themselves (i.e. the school children). This is a truly toxic unintended consequence of an uncritical, unforgiving audit-driven inspection regime; and if inspectors are not aware of these highly distorting dynamics and consequently fail to take them into account in their school judgements, then yet more 'symbolic violence' is very likely to be perpetrated (albeit, perhaps, unwittingly).

Power also challenges programmatic, procedural approaches to risk management, pointing out that 'Research… challenges highly rationalistic models of risk analysis which assume away the important psychological and cultural dimensions of risk understanding' (p. 18). And later, he returns to the vexed question of unintended consequences:

> Despite explicitly stated principles of supporting managed risk-taking and value creation, the deeper bureaucratic logic of internal control represents the opposite. To the extent that internal control-based risk management is over-organised, it is a kind of new religion and *may encourage perverse behaviours* by virtue of the faith it engenders in itself. (Power, 2004, p. 50, my italics)

These latter considerations will be highly relevant to the close analysis that follows.

The preceding discussion, then, forms a necessary and important backdrop to the analysis of the Ofsted report's judgements on the safeguarding issues that now follows.

CLOSURE REPORT

Analysis of the Ofsted Inspection Report

Note: In what follows, and for ease of reference, verbatim quotations from the Ofsted inspection report under scrutiny here are in **bold**. This will make it immediately obvious as to who is saying what in what follows.

In the January 2020 Ofsted inspection report on Wynstones, we read that **'Children are at risk of serious harm and are not protected when they should be'**. This extremely strong and damaging claim masquerades in the report as some kind of objective assessment. Yet no substantive evidence is adduced to support this assertion, except that the 'procedures' that are so central to Ofsted's worldview were allegedly not being followed. This needs unpacking, as it will throw much revealing light on the low-trust, fear-driven safeguarding ideology that underpins and drives Ofsted's practice – and which is embedded in a narrowly instrumental, control-fixated worldview that Steiner Waldorf pedagogy emphatically rejects, and which completely ignores the realities of what Power (2004, p. 50) calls 'the *essential* disorder of organisational life' (my italics). I return to these important issues below.

We read, then, that **'Child protection issues are not dealt with in line with statutory safeguarding requirements'**. And that **'Some staff have not reported serious safeguarding concerns relating to pupils' worrying behaviours'**. Who, precisely, is defining these situations as being 'serious'?; who is claiming to define what 'worrying behaviour' consists in?; and whose subjective judgement is being invoked here, and is being assumed to be *the* correct assessment of the safeguarding situation? Is it written procedures in rule-books (Power's 'proceduralising of risk' – Power, 2004, p. 23) that should be trusted as the best judge of what constitutes a safeguarding situation that warrants investigation and needs acting upon? – or are sentient and professional human beings in specific contexts best placed to make such complex, unique decisions and assessments? These questions go right to the heart of what some authorities view as England's manic, fear-driven and heavily bureaucratised Health, Safety and Safeguarding Culture (hereafter, HSSC), and which I examined at length in the previous section.

Psychotherapist Steve Burchell (2020), for example, has recently looked in depth at the 'shadow' side of safeguarding, how it does not achieve its stated aims, and how it *actively disempowers* both those doing the protecting and those who are seen as needing protection. For Burchell, behind the safeguarding issue is a fantasy that we can save people from hurt – which is an impossibility – and organisations have colluded with this fantasy to the detriment of the professionals themselves and their 'clients' (which, in the current situation, means school children). And here is Michael Power (2004, p. 22), soberingly but realistically pointing out that 'failures and accidents are possible in complex environments, *even with the most competent, ethical and expert oversight possible*' (my italics). It is hardly surprising, then, that 'Political discourses of "zero-tolerance" [as demonstrated by Ofsted in the analysis below – RH] sit uneasily with a risk-based ethos' (ibid.).

Matt Robinson has related concerns to those of Burchell and others, writing that 'The bigger question for me is why we still have so many Education [Health & Safety] systems and cultures that are not fit for purpose. They are too long winded, too focused on micro-hazards or low likelihood risks. ...*They do not engage staff, require thought or encourage openness.*' (Robinson, 2016, my italics). And here is Power again:

> [the] quality assurance model... has been exported to a wide variety of domains and organisational settings.... Such systems have been criticised for being excessively bureaucratic and for *concentrating on auditable process* rather than on substantive outputs and performances. Worse still, *they distract professionals from core tasks* and create incentives for gaming. (Power, 2004, p. 26. my italics)

There also exists a substantial literature that foregrounds the disabling unintended consequences of an over-protective culture towards children, and the harm it does to them (e.g. Furedi, 1997; House, 2003–4; Gill, 2007; Furedi & Bristow, 2008; Brown & Hanlon, 2014; Robinson, 2016) – just some of the many concerns being:

- Children unconsciously experience and incorporate the anxiety of adults around them, and the pervasive cultural and institutional anxiety that saturates the system... – children's mental-health crisis, anyone? (cf. Creasy and Corby, 2019).

- Paradoxically and ironically, making things too safe can actually starve children of the very experiences that best help them learn how to keep themselves safe and healthy (Gill, 2007).

- Teachers and managers become preoccupied with institutional and bureaucratic imperatives, with the threat of legal action overhanging everything, and a sense of being under constant, unremitting surveillance – and in the process they can easily lose the capacity of spontaneously and fully *being with* children in-the-moment. Power again throws much light on this pernicious process:

  > [T]he new style of internal control-focused risk management has created an intensified attention to process, and to the responsibilities of *middle managers **who must constantly create appearances** of process*, via risk mapping and other techniques, in order to defend the rationality of their

decisions. Where this 'risk game' is closely bound up with a 'blame game', *the effect can be highly defensive reactions from organisational participants.* (Power, 2004, pp. 45–6, my bold and italics)

- Any suspect sign, however minor, tends to be assumed to be an instance of abuse or harm until it is proven to be otherwise – which sets in train a series of institutional bureaucratic processes that can easily have a catastrophic impact in all manner of ways – for example in a Steiner school, where children have the emotional continuity of, and the deep attachment to, the same Class Teacher for eight years, and will be devastated, and their education massively disrupted, if they lose that teacher through what proves to have been an unwarranted suspension (which tragically we know has happened in the case of Wynstones). This is an excellent if tragic example of how, with grotesque irony, mainstream HSSC can perpetrate a violence on a pedagogy that differs from the mainstream, when 'the rules' are, to be charitable, less-than-thoughtfully applied.

- A 'low-trust environment' pervades everything and everyone – again, something that all children consciously and unconsciously imbibe into their being.

- More widely, the preoccupation with safeguarding is a culturally embedded artefact of late-modern culture's increasing obsessions with fear, as outlined so convincingly by sociologist Frank Furedi (e.g. Furedi, 2018); and a slavish adherence to procedures and rules around the safeguarding issue fails to engage reflexively with the culturally located and quite possibly transitory nature of these practices, and the negative unintended consequences many claim them to be generating on many levels. In tune with Furedi's work, others have also argued that over recent years there has been an over-intrusion of the State into the private realm, with the subtle state/private balance shifting too far towards intrusion (e.g. Devine, 2018).

Further still, one of the great dangers of the robotic following of rules and procedures that define safeguarding and associated cultures is that *the very existence* of such procedural rules, and their consequent effects, actually interfere with and denude professionals' own capacity to make informed, appropriate judgements in real-life, uniquely contextual circumstances. That is, such bureaucratically loaded procedures *de-professionalise the professionals* – which ironically then renders children *less* safe, because informed, sensitive and autonomous professionals are better custodians of children's safety and well-being than are written rules and protocols (for parallels in the field of counselling and psychotherapy, see House, 1997).

But with Ofsted's low-trust 'proceduralist' approach to safeguarding, there is simply no space for any alternative – possibly less damaging – ways of thinking about these issues. The key point here, of course, is that Ofsted's approach to safeguarding, and the way it enforces it, is just one amongst a number of possible legitimate and defensible approaches; and to be assuming, first, that one's own approach is right and must be adhered to without question, and then if such adherence is not followed, a school is closed by State action, is an authoritarian approach which is unacceptable, and difficult if not impossible to defend in a democratic society in which professionals earn their professional autonomy for very good reasons.

Ofsted's Audit Culture approach to HSSC also uncritically assumes that it is both desirable and possible for professionals to be fully conscious of all they do, and why – and then to be able to articulate this in procedural language. The literature in this field, from authorities like Donald Schön and Guy Claxton, suggests quite the opposite – i.e. that professionals are not by any means always able to consciously articulate what they are deciding and why; and the very demand that they do so actually interferes with and negatively affects their capacity to reach sensitive, contextually appropriate decisions (e.g. Atkinson and Claxton, 2000a, b; Schön, 1984, 1987; see also House, 2017). As Matt Robinson (2016) puts it, 'so many risk assessments and systems seek to lock [simple, natural judgements] down or formalise every last detail, reducing competence and confidence to make those judgements' (my italics). Power agrees: 'the risk management of everything is characterised by the growth of risk management strategies that displace valuable – but vulnerable – professional judgement…' (Power, 2004, pp. 10–11, my italics). And later, in a resounding statement that throws into sharp relief the cultural damage wrought by what he calls the pathology of the 'risk management of everything' ideology, Power argues that:

> society will have more of what it does not really need – certifications and non-opinions which are commonly accepted as useless and which are time-consuming and distracting to produce; and less of what it does – valuable but vulnerable judgements based on the best available knowledge to inform decisions in the face of uncertainty. This is the essential pathology of the risk management of everything. (p. 46)

If this view is anything like right, then it has considerable, if not momentous implications for an organisation like Ofsted, that will often be making judgemental assessments having fateful implications for both the future of teachers' careers and of a school's very existence. Not least, the 'low-trust', procedure- and protocol-dominated ideology dominating the Ofsted approach to HSSC makes it difficult if not impossible to create and sustain a creative space for embodied, professional judgement to prevail. And as psychoanalyst Donald Winnicott showed many years ago, compliance is invariably the death-knell of creativity (see House, 2018a) – and so is almost guaranteed to compromise, if not destroy, the space for creative autonomous judgement that professional teachers need in order to be able to function effectively in living, complex school communities. Power (2004, p. 47) is also withering about the way in which a system demanding compliance necessarily functions in a defensive way:

> the traditional distinction between legal regulation, voluntary codes and organisation-specific rules is not useful; all are effectively experienced by organisational participants 'legalistically' and demand defensive compliance strategies. Even the well-worn distinction between principles and rules does not offer a solution path here; principles will tend to be interpreted legalistically in organisations via in-house manuals….

More specifically, and at worst, Ofsted may well be routinely basing their fateful judgements on at best highly partial, and at worst wholly inadequate perceptions and assessments of the situation in a given school; and so they will sometimes, at least, be condemning schools and teachers based on wholly erroneous pretexts.

Perhaps the key point to emerge from this extended discussion is that those imposing bureaucratic, rule-bound procedures need to understand, first, that there are principled and coherent arguments that challenge many of the procedural minutiae, and sometimes the whole philosophy underpinning, mainstream safeguarding culture; and that many teachers will share those misgivings – and certainly some in the Steiner education movement. Genuine pedagogues have a solemn professional responsibility to maximise the learning offer and the quality of the learning experience they provide for their children – and Steiner teachers take this responsibility very seriously indeed. Given this complex situation, those responsible for safeguarding culture – in this case, Ofsted – have a grave responsibility to understand these complexities, and to behave thoughtfully and proportionately, when faced with a pedagogical and educational culture which has principled and well thought-through objections to the prevailing legally and narrowly enforced safeguarding culture.

I submit that the precipitate closing of a school with over 250 happy and enthusiastically engaged children is decidedly not the way to discharge this grave responsibility.

The key point here is not to argue that the managerialism-critical perspective presented here is necessarily right, and the hyper-vigilant managerialism of the Ofsted approach to safeguarding wrong-headed (though of course I have my views on this). Rather, the key point is that the Ofsted approach is highly contestable – and it is strongly challenged and critiqued in the literature, as discussed earlier. In this situation, it is surely incumbent on Ofsted to display some flexibility and even humility around its preferred practices – and particularly where a substantially different pedagogical approach takes a distinct and principled position on these safety and safeguarding issues. In this report, there is no evidence that any such flexibility and latitude, and an associated deferment at times to principled professional autonomy, have been exercised.

We read further in the inspection report that **'These members of staff have been allowed to continue teaching without disciplinary action to address this dangerous performance'**. This is very grave language to be deploying, and in a report such as this that is making judgements about professionals, it is language that should be used very precisely, rather than in a loose, scatter-gun way. Thus, who, precisely, is taking it upon themselves to deem this 'performance' to be 'dangerous'? Whose unavoidably *subjective judgement* is being invoked here – and is then being treated in the report's narrative as if it is objective, incontrovertible truth? Note also, that Ofsted is demanding 'disciplinary action' – as befits an organisation whose leitmotif is compliance and the enforcing of its own will – and which, moreover, does not facilitate the possibility for disagreeing with it.

Again, we read that **'Leaders do not address or challenge staff behaviour that is unacceptable and places pupils at significant risk'**. At the risk of sounding like a stuck record, who here is judging what is 'unacceptable' behaviour? – the inspectors. And how, precisely, are the highly complex decisions being made by an outsider – with no living understanding of the unique context – as to whether pupils are being placed **'at significant risk'**?

We are then told in the report that the behaviour and anti-bullying policies published on the school's website **'do not promote good behaviour or prevent bullying'**. This statement again betrays the simplistic HSSC ideology in which Ofsted is uncritically immersed. Policies *qua policies* can never 'promote good behaviour', or 'prevent bullying' – this is a complete misunderstanding and misrepresentation of the dynamics of actual human relationships. The reader is referred to the excellent work of Gill (2007), Furedi and Bristow (2008) and Brown and Hanlon (2014) for chapter-and-verse on Health and Safety Culture, and the way in which, paradoxically and counter-intuitively, it actually renders the kind of abuse that it is intended to prevent *more* likely to occur (see also my earlier discussion on this).

Next, we read that **'There is little evidence to suggest that staff follow, implement, or understand these policies well enough'**. If my argument is correct that policies per se can never either create good behaviour or prevent bullying (though of course they do have the effect of making *us* feel better because we can convince ourselves, individually and institutionally, that we are *doing something* about it), then this statement that the inspectors are deploying in their report as a criticism of school staff becomes meaningless.

We are then told that **'*Many* families leaving the school have cited safeguarding concerns or bullying as the reason'** (my italics). Note that we are not told how many families constitutes 'many'… – is it 10? – 20? – 50?... – for without actually specifying the order of magnitude of this problem, this is a very loosely worded insinuation to make about such a grave issue. Ofsted must presumably know exactly how many families and children this includes – and if they don't, they're failing to walk their own 'Audit Culture talk' here.

We are told further that **'Some parents report that they have not been able to share concerns that their child is being bullied *due to the relationships that exist between other parents and/or staff*'** (my italics). It is difficult to know what this statement means. What are the 'relationships' that are being invoked here? – and how do whatever those 'relationships' consist in make it difficult for parents to report bullying concerns?

Next, we read that **'There are records of poor behaviour and bullying from September 2019, when a new system was introduced'**. Again, there is a crucial issue of definition here, and also the tacit, unarticulated assumptions that are tied up with the inspectors' chosen discourse. Who, precisely, has the authority and objectivity unequivocally to define what constitutes 'poor behaviour'? – the inspectors, it seems; and perhaps even more presciently, who is making the assumption that 'poor behaviour' should never occur? As the great paediatrician and psychoanalyst Donald Winnicott said, paradoxically naughtiness is often not only necessary, but is *a developmental achievement* for at least some children. We need far more sophisticated and subtle (psychoanalytically informed) understandings of child behaviour than is shown by this superficial Ofsted approach to what are complex issues.

We then read that **'There is no evidence that leaders have oversight of these [policies] or that sanctions have been applied in accordance with the school's policies'**. Again, who precisely is assuming that 'sanctions' are necessarily the appropriate way to respond to (allegedly) 'poor' behaviour? This punitive approach is Ofsted's, and it is not necessarily shared by a phalanx of experts and authorities on child development and behaviour – nor, for that matter, by Steiner Waldorf teachers.

Next, we are told that **'There is little in place to support pupils with challenging behaviour'**. What is being referred to here? And are good 'quality human relationships' with sensitive teachers being assumed to be insufficient in this regard?

Next, **'there is no evidence that [external guidance to try to reduce bullying] has led to fewer bullying incidents'**. This is evidently presented by the inspectors in their report as some kind of criticism. Yet who is assuming the authority to define what 'bullying' actually consists in? Also, the problem with this kind of mechanistic thinking is that by assuming that a simple quantitative reduction in easily categorisable 'bullying' incidents constitutes a success and a step towards a more civilised school, this completely ignores the phenomenon that such 'shadow' behaviour, when legislated away by rules and protocols without addressing the deep causes, simply gets redistributed elsewhere in the system. Put differently, invoking a simple metrics-orientated 'number of bullying incidents' (as Ofsted commonly does) does not begin to grapple with the complexity of what 'bullying', and its transformation, actually consist in. For example, it ignores the crucial *psychodynamic* aspects and institutional complexities of 'bullying', with its deeply unconscious victim/persecutor dynamics (Hall, 1993; Karpman, 2004; Weinhold & Weinhold, 2017), and so on. So to invoke simple headline metrics of this kind in order to criticise the school is again inadequate, as the 'evidence' adduced by Ofsted isn't sufficient to justify the critical judgement they are making on this issue.

In passing, one might also ask whether Ofsted's own behaviour as the school inspectorate watchdog could be construed as 'bullying', as some authorities and educational critics have claimed going right back to its early leadership under the late Chris Woodhead in 1992 (e.g. Jeffrey & Woods, 1996). I have heard one school parent say, 'Ofsted *are* the safeguarding issue in this country'. And in the questionnaire report presented in the appendix to this book, another parent writes, 'This bullying organisation have [sic] ruined our school'.

Yet these are not loose, casual accusations. Organisations commonly develop a culture that is deeply embedded by their founders; and the intimidatory reign of unremitting surveillance and enforcement that Ofsted has cultivated was well expressed by Woodhead when, at the height of his powers, he said in a BBC TV interview: '[Ofsted] is a very fine, sharp instrument… We will be exposing inadequate provision wherever we find it. And where provision is inadequate, we will be reporting it loudly and clearly' (BBC1 Lunchtime News, 2 August 1999). If there is anything in this contention, then there are grave questions to be answered about the *unconscious institutional dynamics* that might be being influenced by an assessment and accountability enforcement organisation that might itself include a bullying ethos. But this is a conversation that goes well beyond this book.

Next, '**…accident records <u>do not always</u> <u>confirm</u> how an injury was obtained, nor describe in detail the nature of the injury. This <u>could</u> lead to concerns about recurring injuries, unexplained injuries or non-recurring injuries, unexplained injuries or non-accidental injuries being missed'** (my underlining). Notice the questionable deployment of the uncertainty-generating but studiously unspecific phrases '*do not always* **confirm**' and '*could* **lead**'. Again, how many actual instances are being spoken of here? – and were those teachers who did not record injuries in this way asked why they didn't do so? That is, why were they not given the opportunity to account for and justify their professional judgement? Or again, is bureaucratic procedure assuming to trump professional judgement? (cf. my earlier discussion on this issue) And where is any evidence presented that actual / additional / avoidable harm *did actually* occur? And if it didn't, what, precisely, is the issue that is a cause for censure here?

We then read that '**Staff did not act to ensure that a child was not injured following an accident. This lack of first aid <u>may</u> have left a child with an untreated injury from when the accident occurred in the early morning'** (my underlining). Note again the crucial word 'may' here. But presumably this didn't actually happen. So again, what is the issue here? It is an invalid criticism to condemn someone for something that *could* have happened but didn't. It could even indicate inspectors (and of course this is speculative and necessarily circumstantial) fishing around for pretexts with which to make criticisms – and/or who were determined to discover what they had *already decided* were features of this school.

Next, we read that '**Leaders have not challenged staff who have put pupils at <u>serious</u> risk due to a lack of supervision. This means that this unacceptable practice can continue and the recent training in supervision that staff have had is**

undermined' (my underlining). Note here the invoked discourse of 'risk' – indeed, '*serious*' risk (cf. Power, 2004). And the assumption that 'supervision' is somehow appropriate and necessary – another classic example of the 'low-trust' environment referred to elsewhere. Yet for Creasy and Corby (2019), this is an issue about the 'taming of childhood' which, for them, is doing such damage to children's development. In their view, we urgently need to 'recognise that children are quite capable of playing on their own, *without adult direction and/or supervision*' (2019, p. 134, my italics).

The inspectors' criticism here is therefore either ignoring or misunderstanding the pedagogical environment that Steiner Waldorf seeks to create – and for which many, if not most, parents informedly choose this education over a mainstream educational approach that is saturated with low-trust, fear-driven surveillance practices, and its accompanying ideology. (As previously mentioned, I know of at least two parents who explicitly chose Wynstones School for their child because it was what they saw as a 'high-trust' environment – and who were dismayed and appalled once all manner of Ofsted-imposed changes were made at the school which, for them, fatally compromised that high-trust ethos in which they wanted their children to thrive.)

Next, the inspectors write that **'At break times, staff <u>do not supervise pupils effectively. It was not evident to inspectors</u> what boundaries were in place or what the agreed expectations of pupils' behaviour are'** (my underlining). Again, highly contestable assumptions about child behaviour are being made here, as well as about supervision. Who is claiming to be the authority on what constitutes adequate and appropriate supervision? Moreover, did any major problems occur that would not have happened if 'supervision' had been in place? And if not, then I maintain that this criticism has no substance.

In Steiner Waldorf education, there is an aspiration to *trusting* children, and not to over-supervise them or over-intrude into their worlds. This is a fundamental pedagogical and philosophical difference from mainstream schooling ideology, of which the inspectors are either not aware – or if they are, they are choosing to ignore it.

The statement that something 'was not evident to inspectors' also makes all manner of contestable assumptions about, first, what constitutes valid 'evidence', and secondly, assuming that *absence of evidence* (as defined, crucially, by Ofsted's approach) constitutes *evidence of absence*. The latter cannot by any means be assumed to be the case – and for this reason alone, this is an invalid criticism unless supported with far more evidence and philosophical justification than are provided in the inspection report. That is, this criticism has the status of mere assertion and surmise; and yet it is presented in this inspection report as a serious and legitimate criticism.

The inspectors also state that **'...unsafe behaviour remains unchallenged'**. Again, who is defining what constitutes 'unsafe' behaviour here? – the inspectors; and according to what philosophy and rationale? Unless the latter are spelt out clearly, and then what was observed in the school shown to diverge substantially from this definition, again this is mere assertion masquerading as legitimate criticism. Indeed, in my perception it is common throughout the inspection report to find these kinds of criticisms 'looking for a hook to be hung on'.

This might sound like a grave accusation to make. Yet it is not as if Ofsted doesn't have form on this issue. In the case of Muslim schools and alleged 'extremism' (the so-called 'Trojan Horse' affair in Birmingham), for example, Arthur (2015) has recently argued that 'The fact that OFSTED inspection reports commented on these activities without placing them within the broader ethos of the schools is problematic and may be interpreted as *inspectors looking for reasons to paint a poor picture of these schools'* (p. 320, my italics). And later (p. 323), we read that

> Inspectors questioned the girls on whether they knew any gay people and whether they had a boyfriend and whether they had friends from other religions. Some believe that the very nature of these questions is extreme and that OFSTED *was not respecting the religious ethos of faith schools, indeed that these inspections were antithetical to their faith and undermined the whole basis of faith schools.* Some would go further and suggest that *inspectors were trying to impose a secular worldview that challenged the religious commitment of believing children.* (my italics)

And with direct relevance to this counter-report, finally, Arthur maintains that OFSTED had 'gone beyond the regulations allowing varying interpretations of inspectors who then go on to inspect and measure compliance to these interpretations' (p. 326, my italics)

So the key point here is that other researchers have previously claimed that Ofsted inspectors have effectively been 'a law unto themselves' regarding the assessments they have made of schools. So it is by no means fanciful to suggest that the same could have happened in relation to Wynstones School – though of course it is an evidential, empirical question as to whether it has occurred in this case or not.

We then read the condemnatory judgement that **'The risk assessment policy is not fit for purpose'**. But for what 'purpose' is it not fit? And who has the right or the authority to define what constituting 'fit for purpose' should look like? – the inspectors…

Next, **'[The risk assessment policy] does not make clear that staff always need to be vigilant and proactive to safeguard pupils and promote their wellbeing.'** This is a highly contestable statement that contains all manner of problematic assumptions. First, why should staff **'always be vigilant and [always be] proactive'**? Such a view again connotes a low-trust ideology that Waldorf pedagogy squarely rejects – and ignores *the unconscious impact on children, and on the whole milieu and relational environment, of being surrounded by adults who are assuming that the children should and need to be under constant and unremitting surveillance* (as discussed earlier in relation to HSSC).

Moreover, even if we accept the premise of this statement, why is it being assumed that teaching professionals need to be told *by a written policy* that they 'always need to be vigilant' – and that if a written policy hasn't spelt this out to them, they either won't be vigilant because a written policy hasn't told them they need to be, or they won't be capable of using their own common-sense professionalism to make appropriate decisions as to the ongoing monitoring of children? Bluntly, this is procedure-*itis* and *de-professionalisation* at their worst, with the rules and procedures ideology, and the culture of fear underpinning it, having taken such a hold that a sensible stance towards policy-making has been lost, with dedicated professionals ending up being at best infantilised, and at worst treated like idiots.

Moreover, it is ironically this kind of attitude to 'procedure' that will end up generating the very opposite of its intention (the well-known 'sat-nav syndrome'), with teachers coming to rely upon such written protocols and thereby losing their intrinsic capacity to be autonomous, sensible professionals (Atkinson & Claxton, 2000a, b). Wastell et al. (2010) have explained at length how the Audit Culture and control-fixated managerialism have lead to disempowerment and the erosion of professional autonomy. In their ethnographical research they examined how social workers organise their practice in an atmosphere of performance management, discovering clear tendencies for attenuated discretion, which reflected the shift to a managerial model of control. They write of

> obvious anxieties about the erosion of professional discretion.... Of concern is the emergence of a pattern of formally conformant behaviour in which the letter of the organisational law is obeyed but without genuine commitment.... While showing up the absurdities of excessive managerial power, such behaviours are ultimately dysfunctional for the organisation.... with the loss of professional agency... mean[ing] that the ability of social workers to deliver the service they desire professionally, in the interests of their clients, has been compromised *by the bureaucratic arrangements to which they are obliged to conform.* (pp. 310, 311, my italics)

As Finnish educationalist Pasi Sahlberg (2012) succinctly puts it, 'accountability is what remains when responsibility is taken away'. It is also not going to help Ofsted–school and Ofsted–teacher relations one bit to infantilise and insult teachers' professionalism in this way – but this can easily be one impact of such procedures.

Moreover, from where is the assumption emanating that it is staffs' responsibility to 'promote [children's] wellbeing'? The very idea that adults have the responsibility to *promote* children's well-being is non-sensical from a humanistic-existential approach to, and a Steiner Waldorf perspective on, learning and education – yet it is being used here, yet again, as a pretext for criticising the school and its policies and staff. And to repeat: even if we were to accept that these *are* valid stipulations (which I don't accept that they are), why is it being assumed that *a written policy* needs to spell these things out to responsible professionals? – and then a school is yet further penalised when it doesn't?

Next, we read that '**The scope of risk assessments is too limited**'. Whose world-view and which body of knowledge are being invoked in order to make this criticism? And were questions asked of the school regarding their own justification for their chosen range of stipulated risk assessments, in order to give them the opportunity to justify its scope? – and if not, why not?

Next, '**Risk assessments are not in place for some vulnerable pupils to help reduce their dangerous behaviours or safeguarding risks. These pupils continue to be at significant risk of harm**'. Again, these are seemingly not criticisms of mal-occurrences that have *actually happened*, but criticisms for something that *might conceivably* have happened – but didn't. Notice, also, the assumed direction of causality – i.e. that a child will be '**at significant risk of harm**' *because of* the absence of a written risk assessment policy. Again, this leaves completely out of account the contextual professionalism and professional responsibility of teachers and staff, and their own capacities, competencies and thoughtfulness in making such decisions. As educationalist Max van Manen has shown only too well, pedagogical and educational thoughtfulness is one of the first casualties of a narrow Audit Culture mentality (van Manen, 1991; see also van Manen, 1986). The superficiality and crude instrumentalism of such fateful judgements are thus again evident.

Next, the inspectors write that '**The designated safeguarding lead was unable to confirm what action had been taken to respond to welfare concerns about children. As a result, potential risks for children have not been reduced and require urgent attention**'. This is a non-sequitur. That the safeguarding lead was unable to state what actions had been taken does not mean *either* that no effective action *was* indeed taken, *or* that such actions were necessary and appropriate in the first place. Moreover, the inspectors then go on to assert that 'potential risks for children have not been reduced' – yet this is a criticism built on the sand of the preceding erroneous statement, on which this further criticism depends, and from which it has been deduced. Yet again a school is being condemned for what *could* have happened but didn't, rather than for what actually did happen – which is quite possibly nothing of adverse note at all. And if anything of an adverse nature *did* occur, it needs to be spelled out in detail by the inspectors – and no such information is given in their report.

Next, '**There is *a lack of independence* in dealing with concerns**' (my italics). This is an interesting statement coming from an organisation – Ofsted – about which significant concerns have been raised about its own complaints procedure (Office for Standards in Education, 2018) – see, for example, Kerr (2017) and Roberts (2020).

Next, we read that '**Furthermore, the published complaints procedure does not show that leaders understand the need to make provision for an**

independent person to act as a member of any complaints panel'. To the extent that the school had an inadequate complaints procedure, this was clearly not acceptable. However, the above is a procedure-centric statement and judgement, where written procedure is assumed to take some kind of hallowed position of 'divine precedence' over human professional relationships and practices. Did the inspectors directly ask the school leaders whether their *actual practice* in the course of a complaints process is to include an independent member on such panels? – and if not, why not? No, what is and is not *in writing* seems to be taken as holy writ, with which to then generate pretexts for copious critical judgements.

Next, we read that **'Parents do not feel able to raise concerns formally or informally'**. This assertion is wholly unacceptable as it stands. It implies that parents *as a generality* feel unable to raise concerns; yet on the say-so of how many parents, exactly, was this generality based? In order to justify such a statement, the inspectors would have needed to canvas the views of the vast majority of parents on this question, and got the answer that most parents did indeed not feel able to raise concerns. Did the inspectors do this? – and if they did, where is the evidence? And if they did not, this statement, as cast in the report, constitutes little more than a smear on the school.

Next, **'The high number of parents removing their children from the school this academic year — particularly those that cite safeguarding and bullying as the reason for this — demonstrates this'**. Again, this is an unacceptable statement. First, precisely how many constitutes the 'high number' being cited here? And how many specifically **'cite safeguarding and bullying as the reason'**? This is an issue that I highlighted earlier, and it constitutes a loose and potentially misleading phrase to use in this context without actually specifying the numbers involved. It is a known consequence of the 'inadequate' grading of a school that a significant number of parents leave (as Ofsted acknowledges in their own report, *Fight or Flight? How 'Stuck' Schools Are Overcoming Isolation: Evaluation Report* (Ofsted, 2020); yet they wish to imply disingenuously in the above wording that it is due to dissatisfaction with the school rather than partly, if not largely, of Ofsted's own doing.

Secondly, just because parents name 'bullying' and 'safeguarding' as their reason for leaving a school, it is an open question as to whether some, most or all of those concerns are valid and justified. They may be, of course – but in the absence of firm confirmation of this, Ofsted inspectors have no justification for using this surmise as a pretext for yet again criticising this (or any other) school. Relatedly, there is a well-known phenomenon of malicious, vindictive and/or score-settling complaints – and before making this judgemental assertion based on what might be hear-say 'evidence', Ofsted would have to do the necessary investigations to satisfy itself beyond all reasonable doubt that the complaints being made were not vexatious. Were these investigations carried out? – and if not, why not?

It also appears that it is legitimate to take the word of parents uncritically, but not to take the word of dedicated working professionals. A guiding ideology that assumes 'guilty until proven innocent' is not an approach that should have any place in Ofsted's fateful assessment of schools, and the far-reaching consequences they generate.

Next, we read that **'Complaints records are incomplete. They do not show how a complaint was resolved, the action taken by the school or the findings of any investigation'**. Again, this is a written records-centric criticism. Do the inspectors have any evidence of *actual complaints* that were not dealt with properly and with due diligence and care? If they do, why are they not detailed, or at least mentioned, in the inspection report? And if not, again here we seemingly have a criticism and judgement based solely on paper work and written records – a *leitmotif* of the bureaucratic Audit Culture, of course, that many argue has no place in our schooling system, and which is again underpinned by an uncritical embracing of an all-pervasive 'culture of fear' in which The Paper Trail and the meticulous recording of everything take precedence, and become the privileged – and sometimes even the sole – metric by which schools are assessed and judged. More generally, I have recently written at length about the problems of the so-called 'Metric Society' (House, 2019-20), and many of these criticisms are painfully evident in Ofsted's Audit Culture approach to assessing school communities.

Power (2004, p. 47) pulls no punches when describing the impact of compliance-oriented record keeping, and its impact on the capacity for professional judgement:

> The consequences of defensive record-keeping for professional judge-ment are potentially catastrophic.... Already, concepts of 'defensive' medicine and auditing are spoken of, *signalling a withdrawal of individ-ual judgement from the public domain.* Minimal records are kept, staff are cautioned about the use of email, and normal correspondence is lit-tered with disclaimer paragraphs. (my italics)

To be reaching what will often be fateful judgements about a whole school based on whether they have correctly ticked the boxes of what many see as being a 'catastrophic' compliance culture is something that needs deep reflection on the part of any organisation enforcing such a culture.

Next, we read that **'The school's culture is detrimental, prohibitive and damaging to <u>any work</u> to safeguard and promote pupils' welfare and well-being. There are fundamental failings that place children at risk of serious harm'** (my underlining). It is a challenge to maintain a level of cool detachment when reading this extraordinary statement. First, it is claiming that the school's 'culture' (whatever that term might mean and connote) **'prohibits *any* work'** (my italics) to either safeguard or promote children's welfare and well-being. We could easily be in the territory of 'the smear' again here. To be blunt, my deconstruction of the vast majority of critical judgements in the report gives the lie to this extraordinary assertion.

The assertion is, moreover, directly contradicted by actual experience on the 'ground floor' by parents and children themselves. The following statement by parents in two different families, for instance, is not unique (taken from the appendix to this book):

> 'From our point of view the school was a good one and we had full confidence in the teachers and the safety of the children who loved the school and were happy for their first six years to run into school skipping. This contrasts strongly with the experience of many parents I know at other schools who struggle to get their children to school because they are not having a good experience of school.'

> 'He never felt unsafe at Wynstones. None of the 30 to 40 families we know have any first-hand knowledge (let alone adverse experience) of safeguarding issues in general, let alone the specific issues that have ostensibly got Ofsted's alarm bells ringing. None of them felt unsafe before.'

Equally extraordinary is the – again – unsubstantiated claim that **'There are fundamental failings that place children at risk of serious harm'**. No serious or convincing evidence has been presented by the inspectors that supports this brutal assertion. In my view it is a subjective speculation based on a procedure- and rules-centric reading of Wynstones School, that is impossible to either prove or refute because it is based on hypothetical speculation on what *could* or *might* have happened – not what actually *has* happened at the school. As such, it is about as far as one could get from being an 'evidence-based' statement. And actual evidence, such as that from the school parents quoted above, is ignored.

Moreover – and I am under no illusions about the gravity of the following conjecture: there is so much distance between the 'evidence' for the condemnatory judgements that Ofsted's inspectors have presented in their inspection report, and this final condemnatory assessment, that it is difficult not to conclude (as alluded to earlier) that consciously or unconsciously, there could have been a bias towards 'discovering' a vindictive pretext in order to condemn the school, possibly leading to forced closure – with the latter action, moreover, being known to very likely lead to a school such as this one never opening again, or else being taken over by a Multi Academy Trust (MAT) (on academies and Steiner education, see House, 2018b) – an objective which the current government has been known to strongly support.

Finally, we read that **'Leaders have not ensured that standards relating to welfare, health and safety and complaints continue to be met'**. This judgement comprehensively falls apart in the face of the many arguments and counter-criticisms made above. For example, what does the term 'meeting standards' actually mean? This is compliance-centred 'Audit Culture Speak' which, when subjected to careful linguistic analysis, is an Emperor With No Clothes charade, lacking in any substantive meaning in the real world of a living school community.

A Necessary Excursion on the Political Economy of Safeguarding

> It is unrealistic to expect that it will ever be possible to eliminate the deliberate harm
> or death of a child – *indeed no system can achieve this.*
> LORD LAMMY, VICTORIA CLIMBIÉ INQUIRY REPORT, 2003 (MY ITALICS)

It is very important to introduce some factually based political and policy-making context for the vexed and controversial issue of safeguarding – for 'models of practice do not emerge or exist in a vacuum; they are intricately linked to political, economic and social projects' (Featherstone et al., 2012, p. 619). Professor of law Lauren Devine has recently written at great length on this question (Devine, 2018), in her book *The Limits of State Power and Private Rights: Exploring Child Protection and Safeguarding Referrals and Assessments.* In a statement that will shock both social liberals and those favouring a sensitively appropriate balance between State power and private family life, Devine writes that

> All children and families are now intended to be subject to continual State
> surveillance…. Consent is not required for intelligence gathering and all
> families are now subject to surveillance via a plethora of State data bases….
> The relentless profiling is analogous to the type of data collected and stored
> in relation to citizens in the criminal justice system. (2018, pp. 53, 56–7)

Thus, under section 11 of the 2004 Children Act, professionals working with children are required 'to report *any* concerns under the broad concept of "safeguarding"' (ibid., p. 53, my italics). And thus has the demonstrably sensible and realistic view of Lord Lammy, quoted above, been 'marginalised in child protection narratives' (ibid., p. 55). With due cause, perhaps, does McGillivray (1997, p. 10) refer to society being '"beset" by the irrational fears of exploited childhood'; and Nikolas Rose refer to childhood being 'the most intensively governed sector of personal existence' (Rose, 1989, p. 123).

Devine further points out that under current safeguarding law going back to the 2004 Children Act, under section 11 of the Act there have been significant increases in the number of safeguarding referrals to the authorities from professionals and agencies working with children – yet 'there has been no corresponding proportionate rise in the amount of child abuse detected following referral' (p. 54; see also p. 44; and for detailed research evidence, see Devine & Parker, 2015) – something that should gravely concern all policy-makers, State agencies and professionals working with children, in the light of the widely documented damage (referred to earlier) that such unwarranted intrusions into family life can and do cause (the distressing details of which investigative procedure are set out in Devine, pp. 65–6). Devine refers to this as failing to give 'adequate consideration of the adverse consequences of categorising large sections of the population as "risky"' (ibid., p. 44).

Put bluntly, what is arguably a blunderbuss of a safeguarding policy may well be causing far more State-sanctioned abuse *of* families, than it is preventing the abuse of children *within* families – a classic example, perhaps, of how overly and disproportionately controlling policy interventions can commonly bring about precisely the opposite of their original intention.

Devine continues:

> This is achieved via mass surveillance of all families to identify children for referral to local authority children's social care departments. These developments have created an increasingly low threshold for referral, dramatically increasing the number of families referred for assessment by 311 per cent over the past twenty-two years.... The expansion of the level of intrusion... [has] eroded privacy and increased the risk of families becoming stuck in a cycle of continuing intervention once under the State's intensive scrutiny.... This is counter to the aim of the Children Act 1989 to interfere into private family life only where necessary, thus preserving parental autonomy unless there is a real danger of significant harm to a child. (pp. 53–4)

The foregoing discussion is vitally important for providing some context for both the specific Ofsted inspection report under scrutiny in this book, and also for the wider impacts of Ofsted's whole approach to safeguarding. Devine refers to 'the uncertainty that surrounds child protection and safeguarding procedures and practice. *Definitions tend to be vague and wide-ranging...*' (op. cit., p. 28, my italics). And for Wrennall (2010, p. 310),

> the definitions of abuse and Child Protection 'concern' are infinitely expandable.... Almost any narrative event can be construed as a Child Protection 'concern'. There are no clear constraints on the construction of what constitutes transgression or what justifies investigation. Increasing surveillance is permitted as, 'the boundaries of official investigation and intervention become almost limitless... definitions of what constitutes "abuse" are inconsistent, contested and increasingly widely cast.' (Wrennall, quoting Jack, 1997, p. 661).... The boundaries between Child Protection and the far broader term, 'safeguarding children' and the delinquency early intervention agenda, are permeable.

Thus, it is clear based on Devine's and Wrennall's careful analyses that there exists considerable *interpretative latitude* for agencies of the State, and their employees, in terms how they interpret, and then implement, the law on safeguarding; and anyone who claims otherwise, and that the law is clear and unambiguous on these complex questions, is either being disingenuous or is, frankly, deluding themselves. According to Devine, '*Subjective interpretations* of children's behaviour, interpreted as 'signs' of abuse, are also triggers [for referral to the authorities]' (ibid., p. 55, my italics). Yet there is an increasingly prevalent view that what is arguably safeguarding law's over-intrusion and over-surveillance are actually *harming* children and childhood – Devine again:

> data that is based on vague impressions about 'signs' embedded in children's behaviour meant every child subjected to endless scrutiny and recording of their demeanor, attainment and behaviour. This amounts to profiling of every child and inferences drawn about parental behaviour on a grand scale. (p. 67)

And more worryingly still: '...extensive information on children, much of it based on "signs" in children's behaviour..., is recorded, shared and acted upon, *but has remained largely unquestioned* either in relation to its reliable evidence base or as a rationale for interventions' (p. 68. my italics). Here also is Creasy & Corby (2019, p. 95):

Within the UK, the safeguarding agenda constructs the image of a world that is not only intrinsically dangerous, it is populated by dangerous individuals who pose an ever-present threat to children. As a consequence, an exaggerated focus on safety restricts children's activities in spite of any long-term detriment that this may pose to health.

So we can see all too clearly how professionals who work with children – who have an implicit Hippocratic Oath to 'do no harm' to their 'clients' – are placed in an impossible position of *professional cognitive dissonance* by all this: torn between, on the one hand, strictly following safeguarding law to the letter, and on the other, the harm they know its inflexible implementation to be doing, both to falsely reported families and in reinforcing the 'low-trust' culture in which children are growing up more generally. And we can see perhaps why at least some principled, dedicated professionals might be reluctant to collude with such a system, as its highly questionable mass-surveillance practices unfold and expand without challenge.

Creasy and Corby (2019) have pointed out that 'recent developments such as Forest Schools appear to be a response to the over-protection of children, [and] such approaches... *rest upon teachers not exerting unnecessary levels of supervision'* (p. 96, my italics). It would be very interesting to research into Ofsted's inspection judgements around safeguarding in such schools – and whether it has been making the same damning judgements of those schools around this issue as it has recently done of Wynstones School; but this is, alas, beyond the scope of this short book.

Following Devine's arguments, then, Ofsted inspectors are clearly free to bring their own *subjective* judgements as to how they choose to interpret and deploy safeguarding law – which will of course vary in terms of both their own personal issues around child welfare and abuse, and their allegiance to, and interpretation of, Ofsted's Enforcer approach. When this kind of interpretative latitude is couched within the context of the relatively inflexible Audit Culture mentality that is at the core of Ofsted's approach, then one should be forgiven for having grave concerns about the implications of this situation for Ofsted's capacity to reach fair, objective and proportionate views on our schools.

The concerns about safeguarding examined here can also be couched within a wider political and cultural context, which help us to understand more fully what many believe to be the prevailing obsession with safeguarding, and its growth since the 1980s under the political economy and paradigmatic context of *neoliberalism*. Creasy (2020, p. 51), for example, argues that 'politicians who promote the ideas of neoliberalism [and managerialism] have done much which contributes to a reduction in trust in such as social workers and have contributed to change in the way that they work' (one could easily substitute the term 'teachers' for 'social workers' in this quotation, of course). According to Arthur (2015), the notion of 'neoliberalism' is highly contested, without any widely accepted definition. However, he maintains that some key themes can be identified: viz.

Through the neo-liberal lens our understanding of schooling becomes narrowly construed; it is less liberal in the traditional sense and... more instrumental in value with a shift from qualitative to quantitative measures of achievement. There is a clear emphasis on the numerical quantification of educational value and success.

Relatedly, Power (2004, p. 53) also refers to 'The risk management of everything [being] closely related to an ambition to measure everything'.

Returning to neoliberalism, in the historically specific and transitory era of neoliberalism where individualism and individual experience are privileged over 'society', community and the total environment (Parton, 2006; Broadhurst et al., 2009a, b; Creasy, 2020), it shouldn't be surprising that politicians, policy-makers and State agents make decisions that sacrifice the well-being of communities on the basis of an individualistic ideology – something that many believe has happened in relation to the Wynstones community of families in this immediate school closure.

Some historical context for illuminating the growth of 'risk and safeguarding' culture is also instructive. Broadhurst et al. (2009) have clearly shown how much of the current very active (or even hyperactive) concern with safeguarding can be traced back to the New Labour government of 1997–2010. As they point out, New Labour was 'preoccupied... with "risks"' (2009b, p. 8). As Tony Blair himself stated, 'risk management... is now central to the business of good government' (Blair, 2002, p. 2). For Broadhurst et al., this meant that

social problems are being increasingly conceptualized in terms of individuals, families, communities and populations deemed to be 'at risk', with interventions targeted to prevent and or ameliorate these risks. Ultimately the management of risk aims to limit the potential for children and young people to develop persistent and intractable patterns of problem behaviour. (2009b, p. 8).

A focus on risk serves to individualize and personalize the problems and vulnerabilities faced by young people and to cut these off from the social, material and cultural context in which they should be situated. This individualization of social problems also serves to mask the responsibilities that the government owes to those children, and their families, whose lived reality is such that they often lack the means and willingness to become active, economically contributing and law-abiding citizens. (p. 8)

The implication of this specifically political-economic perspective on safeguarding is that schools as institutions are suffering enormously because of the way in which they are being quite unreasonably expected to compensate for, and effectively iron out, the massive socio-economic inequalities in late-modern society; and one consequence of this is the ruthless 'enforcer approach' of quasi-State institutions like Ofsted, who punish any school that does not unquestioningly embrace its ideological commitment to what one might call 'manic safeguarding ideology'.

Let me be absolutely clear what is and is not being said here. Of course it goes without saying that children need to be protected from undue harm in schools. But – and it's a big one

– such protection should be proportionate and realistic, should not completely and largely displace and denude professional responsibility, and certainly should not be being underpinned by an unconscious, unarticulated ideological drive to make up for the gross inequalities in society that are generated elsewhere in the free-market economy. Yet I submit that this is precisely what is happening in terms of the attitude that Ofsted displays and deploys towards safeguarding; and that as a result, schools which do not immediately jump to Ofsted's tune and comply with its unreasonable demands are punished and victimised. I maintain that this process explains, at least in part, what has happened to Wynstones, and also to other Steiner schools which are reluctant to meekly comply with Ofsted's strictures and demands.

Unsurprising, then, when we also read that 'the risk management agenda also has important repercussions for the interactions and interventions that professionals are able to pursue with children and their families' (Broadhurst et al., ibid.). And further,

> Risk management is premised on structured assessment tools which identify and assess 'risk' as a means to determine the level and specificities of the intervention deemed necessary. A focus on risk is seen to increase the consistency and rigour of assessment and to enable practitioners to adopt a more focused approach to intervention. *But the cost of this ideological commitment is huge:* ...this focus can... conflate and indeed, obscure 'needs'. *The risk imperative may also serve to constrain and undermine professional practice and discretion.* (ibid., my italics)

Another key strand to the contextualising political economy perspective maintains that part of the explanation for there being such a heavy emphasis on safeguarding and the 'making safe' ideology in schools is that (as with the expectation that schools must generate social mobility), a quite inappropriate expectation is being placed on the schooling system that it can play a key role in the policing of children's safety and wider, amorphously defined welfare. On this view, it should come as no surprise that the State apparatus will tend to be particularly aggressive and unduly proactive in its desire to 'deliver' safe (and socially mobile) children, as it is endeavouring to make up for what it is quite impossible to deliver through neoliberal free-market mechanisms, and especially so when the alienation, hardship and inequality created by that very system is a major factor generating children's compromised safety – or as Parton (2010, p. 592) puts it: the mainstream approach to safeguarding 'fails to address the over-riding structural inequalities which have a pervasive and direct impact on the full range of "outcomes" experienced by children and young people'.

In similar vein, for Wrennall (2010, p. 316):

> The assumption that better outcomes for children would arise from billion-dollar databases and the 'Care' system, rather than from poverty reduction, housing provision, better schools, safer medical services, better before and after school care, holiday clubs, children's hotels, recreational and leisure services, conflict resolution and mediation services, mentoring, parenting education and Family therapy, is highly questionable.... [A] tenacious class bias... insists that poverty can't be re-duced by money, but can be attacked through punishment.

In the most stark form taken by this line of critique, instead of looking at the fundamentals of the market society itself and its complicity in generating multiple assaults on children's well-being (e.g. Palmer, 2015), data-driven managerialist 'solutions' masquerading as 'safeguarding' and an enforcement organisation (Ofsted) that rides rough-shod over the subtleties of pedagogy are deployed that merely deal with the symptoms and fall-out from the system. And it gets even worse; for in being burdened with the responsibility for 'delivering' safeguarding (and social mobility), teachers then commonly become highly stressed and disorientated by a demand on them that is in principle impossible to achieve.

Such a perspective helps to situate and illuminate the hyperactivity of the State's overweening intrusions around the safeguarding question; and this accounts for why those who can see through these contradictions are distinctly uneasy about the way the bureaucratically aggressive safeguarding issue is being deployed and 'acted out' by institutions like Ofsted. I maintain, therefore, that there needs to be an informed and carefully thought-through political-economic locating of the way safeguarding is bureaucratically configured in late-modern societies.

Moreover, government rhetoric about freeing schools from State (local government) control is argued by Arthur (2015) to be singularly disingenuous – for behind the rhetoric about 'market principles',

> Paradoxically, such policies appear to have increased central government control through a system of standards, testing and measuring watched over by the inspection regime of OFSTED. Government can also issue statutory regulations that seek to govern without specifying exactly what must be done. So while the government claims that schools are being set free, the reality appears to be that there is increasing control over schools from the Department for Education. (Arthur, 2015, p. 313)

Arthur's overall conclusions are damning, with 'The government and its inspection regime prov[ing] inadequate in monitoring the effectiveness and risks contained in implementing neo-liberal policies (2015, p. 324)' and 'The neo-liberalisation of education has had consequences for the governing of schooling producing negative outcomes together with a set of contradictions and paradoxes' (ibid., p. 325). This, then, is the political-economic backdrop to the safeguarding question under close scrutiny here.

Creasy and Corby also make a link between neoliberalism and attitudes to childhood, arguing that 'seeing children as economic becomings contributes to interventions within children's lives which have the effect of taming childhood' (2019, pp. 96–7; cf. Gill, 2007; Palmer, 2015), with risk discourses then uncritically dominating policy-making and the practices of State agents without any consideration being given to the negative unintended side-effects of such a focus.

In sum, the purpose of this discussion is neither to argue for a change in the law (though of course I have my views on that) or to argue that the law of the land on safeguarding should not be upheld. But what I am arguing is that when one adds together: (1) the considerable ambiguity around the law as it stands, in terms of how it is interpreted and the definitions of key terms understood (Devine, 2018); (2) the demonstrably adverse impacts research is now showing narrow legal safeguarding practices to be having on family life; and (3) the grave situation of professionals not being allowed to exercise contextually located judgement and sensitively informed discretion on these questions – then we have a perfect storm of a controversy on how safeguarding ideology can easily be deployed as a disciplining measure by agencies seeking a pretext for so doing.

Whether this latter analysis has direct relevance to the case of the forced closure of Wynstones School on safeguarding grounds is an issue which the reader will need to take a view on, based on the evidence and the arguments presented in this book.

Conclusion

> *Governments and large organisations must always act as if they are in control,*
> *so is risk management simply the new game of reassurance, an audit explosion*
> *in new clothes....?.... [T]here is a functional and political need to maintain*
> *myths of control and manageability, because this is what various interested*
> *constituencies and stakeholders seem to demand. Risks must be made auditable*
> *and governable.*
>
> MICHAEL POWER

> *Ofsted are the safeguarding issue in this country.*
>
> A SCHOOL PARENT

I have spent some considerable time and space addressing the safeguarding question here, as it is seemingly a key pretext given by Ofsted and the DfE for its offensive against England's Steiner schools (as articulated in Amanda Spielman's letter of January 2019, to be examined in the next chapter – Spielman, 2019), and is also the main pretext deployed by Ofsted and the DfE for the forced immediate closure of Wynstones School. Yet as I have shown, there exists a very considerable literature and associated body of critical thinking that cast severe doubt on the appropriateness and sound sense of Ofsted's whole approach to safeguarding – which in turn renders highly problematic, at the very least, its deployment of their proceduralist approach to these issues as a core pretext for the fateful decision by the Department for Education to forcibly close down the school.

Throw into the same cocktail a compliance ideology, a preoccupation with risk and its extinguishing, and an overarching culture of fear, and the result is about as toxic and antithetical to anything approaching effective governance as one could imagine. Here is Michael Power (2004, pp. 47–8) again:

> Despite bold claims for the value-adding potential of risk management, the deeper logic is that of compliance, bordering on paranoia and hyper-defensiveness. As risk language becomes legitimate in organisations, anything can be a risk demanding

attention. And, in this downward spiral, it follows that employees and individuals become their own individualised, defensive risk managers in forms of responsibility aversion and a 'culture of fear' of secondary risk.

White (2009) has looked at what she calls the 'erroneous assumptions' involved in the practice of information-sharing amongst professionals around safeguarding (p. 94), emphasising the complexities inherent in (inter-) professional communication, and arguing that unless such processes are understood to be *interpretative* rather than objectively factual, then effective progress in safeguarding is unlikely to occur. The implications should be obvious in the context of this chapter – viz. that to treat safeguarding in the superficial instrumentalist way that Ofsted commonly does – and certainly in its inspection report on Wynstones School – is to risk chronically misspecifying what is actually happening in this highly complex field – and thence to risk committing gross injustices in the judgements it makes.

The key argument here, then, is not about Ofsted being right or wrong in its approach (though I have my views on that): rather, the question is whether it is a legitimate use of State power when what are demonstrably paradigmatically challengeable views, with which many principled professionals and academics flatly disagree, are used as the rationale for the brutal and non-negotiable decision to close a school virtually overnight. And in closing, one also wonders whether in their condemnatory judgements about teachers, Ofsted ever takes account of Power's important point that 'professionals are often so busy that they can only cope by taking a calculated risk *not* to implement certain procedures' (2004, p. 48, his italics).

CHAPTER 3

School Culture, Leadership, Pedagogy – and Paradigm Incommensurability

In this chapter, I subject the remainder of the Wynstones Ofsted inspection report to a critical analysis, with nearly all of this chapter being confined to such an analysis. Unlike the previous chapter, I have not written major separate sections looking at the contextualising background to the themes examined below, as they have played a lesser role in the closing of the school. Nevertheless, there are important arguments to be made in relation to many of the claims made in Ofsted's judgements and the case they make to support them, and these will be woven into the analysis in what follows, citing relevant literature where appropriate.

School Culture, Leadership and the Staff Body

At the start of the inspection report, we see the tell-tale phrase **'Considerable turbulence, a detrimental culture…'** in describing Wynstones School. We need to ask, 'detrimental' to what? – for this is a loose characterisation that needs far more specific articulation and clarification.

As for 'turbulence', the question immediately arises as to whether the inspectors had considered the possibility that any 'turbulence' that does exist in the school might be an artefact of the impact that the intrusion of practices and worldviews that are alien to Steiner Waldorf pedagogy have had on the school and its community. On this plausible scenario, Ofsted first intrudes into a school community of a fundamentally different pedagogical approach, generating considerable dissatisfaction and 'turbulence' in that community and amongst the staff, and then adversely judges the school for that same turbulence for which its own intrusion may well be responsible.

Little surprise, therefore, that **'turbulence and a detrimental culture'** were critically identified by Ofsted's inspectors in their most recent inspection report – which, once generated by the co-principals' compliance with, and capitulation to, Ofsted's Waldorf-violating demands, were then used as one of the pretexts for criticising and then closing the school.

We also read that **'There is no culture or system to hold teachers to account. Consequently, teachers continue to do as they please.'** This statement says far more about Ofsted's arguably quasi-authoritarian approach to accountability and compliance than it does about the appropriateness or otherwise of teachers' behaviour in Wynstones School. First, are not all teachers accountable for their effect on pupils?

More specifically, it is being assumed here that teachers need to be 'held to account' – an immediate question arising being, 'account' to whom, and for what? – to make them comply with Ofsted's demands, perhaps? And what Ofsted is casually and pejoratively referring to as teachers 'do[ing] as they please' is actually called 'teacher's professional autonomy' in Steiner Waldorf parlance, as well as in many other successful educational systems, such as in Finland. But perhaps professional autonomy is a pedagogical phenomenon that is largely incompatible with Ofsted's ideological worldview, and which they find it very difficult to understand or recognise within Ofsted's entrenched 'regime of truth' (Foucault).

We are also told of '*inherent* **weaknesses in the quality of education. Leaders report that changes are being blocked by a group of *resistant* teachers…**' (my italics and underlining). These are, to say the least, highly problematic terms. First, for the record and as already mentioned, Waldorf schools are not meant to have formally defined 'leaders' and hierarchies of power but, rather, work with a progressive 'distributed leadership' approach. 'Managers' are by no means formal 'leaders' in a proper Steiner Waldorf school; so the language of 'leaders' being conflated with 'managers' constitutes an alien discourse that Ofsted is imposing on the school, which arguably then leads to it making unwarranted assumptions and assertions. (In passing, it is clear that Ofsted is assuming that 'leadership' is all-important (cf. Coffield, 2017, pp. 11–14), yet '[T]here remains to this day no hard evidence of a direct causal relationship between any form of leadership and improved student attainment' – ibid, p.12).

More importantly, Ofsted's term 'resistant' is highly revealing. In reality, a more accurate term would arguably be 'non-compliant'. What seems to have happened here is that a number of teachers in Wynstones School have refused to have the Steiner Waldorf curriculum and ethos undermined and, at worst, hopelessly compromised by Ofsted and the instrumentalist Audit Culture which Ofsted purveys (e.g. Power, 1997; Strathern, 2000a, b; Apple, 2004, 2005 a, b). Put differently, these 'resistant' teachers critically referred to by Ofsted have declined to meekly comply to demands which would, in their view, fatally compromise their professional and ethical commitment to their chosen pedagogy. Of course Ofsted experiences such behaviour as 'resistance' to the will it seeks to impose, but in my own parlance, such ethically driven professional behaviour is much more accurately termed 'Principled Non-compliance' (e.g. House, 2018a).

From all reports, over the past year or two the Wynstones school community has been split asunder by the intrusion of an alien compliance-based high-stakes accountability regime (represented by Ofsted), making very critical judgements about a pedagogical world with fundamentally different values based on collaboration and the professional empowerment and autonomy of teachers. The latter, by no means limited merely to Steiner Waldorf schools and recognised by many educational authorities as essential for the flourishing of the education profession, will be compromised, if not positively harmed, by much of the worldview and associated practices that Ofsted espouses and represents. This is again a theme that will recur in different guises in what follows in this report with respect to Wynstones School.

Another important issue is the *culture of secrecy* that seems to have been apparent in Wynstones School's management. There is a considerable irony here: for normally in a Steiner Waldorf school, there would exist a spirit and practice of non-defensive open-mindedness and open-heartedness. But when subjected to the 'low-trust' Ofsted regime, a knock-on low-trust milieu is consequently generated in which people's delicate capacity to trust in an open, undefended way is often substantially compromised, thence generating a 'culture of fear' (e.g. Furedi, 2018) which can have profoundly damaging effects on the whole culture of a school. Again, I touch on this issue repeatedly in the book.

We then read what is perhaps the most shocking statement of all in the inspection report – namely, that **'The principal summed up inspectors' description of the school's culture as "toxic"'**. One has to ask, first, why is this statement being deployed in the report in this way; and what conceivable relevance does it have if inspectors have been attempting to present an objective report on a school's functioning? No further information is given to contextualise the principal's alleged making of this remark – for example, was it said approvingly, or in a way that demonstrated that he *disagreed* with such a view? Without this information, and without hearing the principal's own explanation of this statement attributed to him by the inspectors, it is difficult not to conclude that this statement has been lobbed into the report in this way in order to buttress Ofsted's required narrative that Wynstones School is indeed 'toxic' – and thence to feed into the DfE's decision to enforce the school's closure.

We then read that **'Relationships between staff and parents and carers have led to a situation where children's safety is secondary to vested interests.'** First, what is meant by the pejorative term 'vested interests' in this context? Is it acceptable for inspectors to deploy damning terms such as this without carefully outlining what they are meant to signify? I need help not to hear this as little more than a smear on the school and its staff – i.e. to accuse it, and them, of putting children's safety at risk in this way, without giving chapter-and-verse on how, precisely, they are claiming this to be occurring.

We are also told that **'The staff body is divided…'**. Of course the school will be 'divided' in the face of a compliance-demanding Ofsted regime that rides rough-shod over the Steiner Waldorf curriculum and pedagogy – with some school staff complying through fear of the retribution they might receive if they don't, and other staff possessing the courage to make a principled stand against what is arguably an attack on their pedagogy and professionalism. And for Ofsted then to deploy this accusation of 'division' to criticise the school, when it is *their own* presence and impositions that have caused the schism in the first place, is unacceptable.

We then read of **'those who want to change [being] intimidated by other staff and a body of parents who want to retain control over the school'**. In my view, such a statement can only emanate from a body – Ofsted – which cannot countenance their compliance agenda being questioned and stood up to. One wonders how often teachers and schools in England find the requisite courage to stand up to and dispute Ofsted's compliance-demanding behaviour. So again, in those cases when it does occur, in my own parlance it is far more appropriately termed 'Principled Non-compliance' (House, 2018a) than it is 'resistance'.

So to transform Ofsted's discourse for a moment, what **'...want[ing] to retain control over the school'** actually means in practice is to protect the integrity of the Steiner Waldorf curriculum from Ofsted's apparent determination to ride rough-shod over it – and to stop the school falling under the control of an Ofsted-imposed Audit Culture ethos that would effectively destroy Waldorf education. Put in this way, wanting **'to retain control over the school'** does indeed sound very different to the way this language is being deployed in Ofsted's inspection report.

In light of all this, then, we should find it of no surprise that in a public letter dated 31 January 2019 written by Ofsted head Amanda Spielman to the then Education Secretary of State, Damian Hinds, Spielman (2019) revealingly wrote of 'questions about whether… common failures [of the Steiner schools] are a result of *the underlying principles* of Steiner education'. It is important at this juncture to analyse this letter further, as it provides important context to what has happened in this inspection and forced school closure.

Spielman claims in the letter that:

> Across the state and independent sectors, there is a wide variety of educational philosophies, and successful schools can be run in a variety of ways. *Ofsted does not have a preferred model.* However, there are fundamentals that need to be in place: good governance, clear lines of responsibility and effective safeguarding procedures. (my italics)

And then a bit later: 'I therefore urge you to consider and further investigate why so many of the Steiner schools inspected are neither protecting children adequately nor giving them *a good standard of education.*' (my italics)

I submit that it is disingenuous for Ms Spielman to claim that Ofsted does not have a preferred educational philosophy, when it enforces all kinds of practices, including pedagogical intrusions, on to England's schools. Everything Ofsted does, with its compliance-demanding, Audit Culture-driven, outcomes-obsessed approach flies in the face of this claim to 'have no preferred [educational] model'. Much of the latter will be all too clear from reading this counter-report. Yet this is the claim being deployed by Ofsted to enable and legitimise what many believe to be a full-frontal assault on Steiner Waldorf schools – including, as Spielman demands of the Department for Education, 'carry[ing] out a thorough examination of the underlying principles of Steiner education and consider[ing] the extent to which they may have contributed to the common failures we found in our inspections, and take action as appropriate'; and 'tak[ing] *enforcement action* to close down all inadequate Steiner schools that fail to improve rapidly' (my italics). So, Ofsted as the self-styled 'enforcer'.

The language here is crystal-clear and, frankly, brutal; yet the pretext given in Spielman's letter for this attitude to the Steiner schools doesn't stand up to critical scrutiny.

In passing, it should also be pointed out that many of the phrases and arguments used in Spielman's letter of January 2019 *are reproduced virtually verbatim* in Ofsted's Wynstones inspection report of a year later, January 2020. What might this be signifying? At the very least, it is consistent with the view that far from the Wynstones inspection report being a fair and objective description of the school as it actually was, with inspectors coming into the school with an appropriately and *professionally essential* open mind, it is, rather, a document that might well be revealing how inspectors went into the school *already having decided* what was going to be wrong with the school – and then hey presto, 'discovering' those very things. Those familiar with the intricacies of research methodology in the social sciences will recognise this phenomenon – and how any remotely capable research committee would laugh out of court any research approach that generated self-confirming data of this nature.

Thus, any reputable academic researcher with even a modicum of understanding of the biasing dangers inherent in research and evaluation would drive a coach-and-horses through the methodological legitimacy of the Ofsted inspection report, given the highly politicised background against which it has been generated (as revealed by Spielman's letter), and the seeming failure to have carefully positioned safeguards in place in their inspection process to ensure against such self-confirming bias.

More specifically, Ofsted routinely seems to be taking no account of two particularly massive sources of bias in their evaluation process. First, there is the argument that what inspectors 'see' tells us far more about them, and the pre-decided and fixed ideological agenda that they are importing into inspections, than it does about the actual educational communities on which they are reporting. And secondly, Ofsted seems to take no account of the fact that much of what they do 'see' (and then evaluate and judge) will be phenomena which have been substantially distorted (or even generated) *by their own presence*, and all that goes with that. This is the well-known phenomenon of the (scientific) observer affecting the field they are observing simply by virtue of their observing it. As I have written elsewhere, 'Ofsted's implicit assumption that the very presence of the inspector does not fundamentally change that which s/he is assessing through his/her (often intimidating) presence is patently absurd' (House, 2000).

If anyone has any doubts about the emotional impact on teachers of an Ofsted inspection, a quarter century ago Woods and Jeffrey (1996) discovered devastating impacts in their detailed research project:

> the technicist approach of an Ofsted inspection impacted against the hol-istic and humanistic values of the teachers, producing a high degree of trauma among them…; [I]nspection… had a latent function of deprofes-sionalisation. Professional uncertainty was induced, with teachers experi-encing confusion, anomie, anxiety and doubt about their competence. They also suffered an assault on their personal selves [which]… took the form of dehumanisation, the loss of pedagogic values… and weakened commitment…. The inspection induces a trauma which penetrates to the innermost being of the teacher. (pp. 325, 340)

Moreover, one understandable response to such circumstances was that teachers typically tried 'to avoid such negative trauma… by shifting identity and status from professional to technician' (p. 325). Or in other words, inspected teachers attempted to recast their professional and personal identity (the two being closely intertwined) to fit the mechanistic technocratic teaching values which the Ofsted 'standards' regime demands – and, indeed, itself models through its didactic, compliance-demanding surveillance practices.

In view of these arguments, any idea that the inspection report under scrutiny here is somehow an objective, fair appraisal of Wynstones School is at best highly problematic; or at the very least, it has to be demonstrated with far more evidence and argumentation than the report currently contains.

Next, we read that **'There is no impartial oversight from trustees. They are all directly connected to the school, staff or parents.'** This is common practice in Steiner schools, which, had the inspectors informed themselves about Steiner Waldorf pedagogy (e.g. by reading Woods et al., 2005), they would have been acquainted with. The notion of 'impartiality' in this specific context only becomes an issue in the low-trust milieu that Ofsted assumes as a default position (as referred to earlier). In a Steiner Waldorf context, by contrast, which places integrity and open-heartedness at its core, full *participatory, co-creative involvement* is seen as a positive advantage and a virtue, not a biasing or compromising shortcoming. Of course this is arguable – and there are strong arguments that can be made on both sides of this question. But that very fact makes it singularly inappropriate for Ofsted to assume that its own favoured view on 'impartiality' is right, and other equally strongly held views on this issue are necessarily wrong – and thence exploiting this question to generate yet another pretext for criticising the school.

Lastly in this section, we are told early on in the inspection report that **'Most middle leaders have stepped down from their roles due to frustrations at the pace of improvement...'**. One wonders, where is the empirical evidence to substantiate this very strong claim? Are these views that were gleaned from interviews with those 'middle leaders' themselves? It certainly will not be sufficient for Ofsted to claim that these views were heard from the school's managers (whom Ofsted terms 'leaders' – see above). Based on the Ofsted report and my analysis of it here, it seems likely that to the extent there were such 'frustrations', they would have been experienced by those Ofsted-compliant teachers who were prepared to capitulate without question to the demands for change being made by Ofsted. In contrast, those teachers who were committed to defending the integrity of the Steiner Waldorf curriculum from those aspects of Ofsted's demands that would have done a symbolic 'violence' to the Waldorf curriculum, had they been uncritically embraced, would doubtless tell a very different story.

Pedagogy and Curriculum

We are then told that **'The curriculum *is not demanding enough* for pupils...'** Now the notion of a curriculum needing to be 'demanding' is a pedagogically contestable claim that is making all manner of assumptions about pedagogy and the way children learn, and the resolution of which turns on how we configure the term 'demanding'. It is an illegitimate move to assert uncritically that because one's own ideology around demanding-ness is not being met, that the school being so judged is necessarily deficient. Yet this is precisely the unwarranted move that the inspectors are making in this simplistic judgement. Did the inspectors have conversations with the teachers themselves about this question, to discover, and possibly learn from, their take on it? And if not, why not?

Further, we read that **'It does not meet the ages, aptitudes and needs of pupils...'**. The Steiner Waldorf curriculum is based on in-depth studies of, and consciously working with, the physical, emotional, intellectual and spiritual development of the growing human being. Both Steiner-based teachers and many professional (non-Waldorf) educationalists have expressed concerns about the age-inappropriate and often too-early imposition of learning methods and goals within the National Curriculum (e.g. House, 2011), even detailing the harm this may be doing to children. This crucial issue, on which there exists a considerable academic and professional literature, is given no attention by the inspectors. Why not?

Next, we read that **'These [curriculum] plans [for English and mathematics] have still not had a discernible impact on pupils' knowledge and understanding'**. What is the evidence for making this judgement, and how are inspectors able to make this bold claim? In making it, they are assuming that learning is procedural, measurable and conscious; yet there is a considerable literature on the *psychodynamics* of learning which convincingly shows that not only is much learning *un*conscious, but indeed, the *most important* aspects of learning are unconscious (see, for example, Neville, 1989; Claxton, 1997a, b, c; Salzberger-Wittenberg et al., 1999; Davou, 2002; Dover, 2002; Hanko, 2002; Saltzman, 2006; Mayes, 2009). On this view, the very idea that procedural *plans* can and will have 'a discernible impact on knowledge and understanding' is to fundamentally misunderstand and mis-specify the nature of the human learning process. In light of these crucial considerations, I submit that the judgement of the school as quoted above is at worst unsustainable, and at best 'not proven'.

Next, we read that **'Leaders have not developed a curriculum that builds pupils' learning effectively over time. They do not yet fully understand all of the weaknesses that underpin the curriculum.'** This assertion is contestable at a number of levels. First, who is claiming the authority to assert that 'weaknesses underpin the (*Waldorf*) curriculum'? And what criteria of assessment are being deployed in making such an assumptive judgement? There is also the Ofsted-centric assumption that in a Steiner school, it is the role of the 'leaders' (for which, read 'managers') to 'develop a curriculum'. One might plausibly speculate that the school's 'leaders' (under surveillance and compliance-inducing pressures?) could easily have given the inspectors the false impression that they *do* indeed possess this power to 'develop' the curriculum.

Yet this is a fundamental misunderstanding and misrepresentation; for in a Steiner school, the curriculum is a given (having been developed in the course of almost a century of Waldorf practice the world over), based on in-depth insight into child development, as noted earlier, with class and subject teachers being given professional and creative autonomy to deliver that curriculum in accordance with their own professionalism, and according to the unique group of children they are teaching. For Ofsted, however, this pedagogical approach is, as Hamlet said to Horatio, 'undreamt of in [their] philosophy'; and so they are singularly ill-equipped to make any judgements about it – and especially when they do not seem to have informed themselves about the key differences between Steiner and mainstream pedagogy before their inspection of the school (a key issue throughout this counter-report).

We are further told that **'There is still no *reading strategy* in place'** (my italics). Yet what does the term 'reading strategy' mean and connote? What we see here is a mainstream-education curricular view of reading being inappropriately imposed on to the Waldorf curriculum – again, a theme that recurs throughout this counter-report. I see no evidence anywhere that these inspectors have informed themselves about the distinctive and pedagogically sophisticated approach to literacy in the Steiner Waldorf curriculum (see, for example, Allanson & Teensma, 2018).

The Ofsted report then refers to **'…recent appointments with some expertise in English and mathematics'** having **'not yet had an impact on the quality of education'**. Again, who precisely is claiming the authority to be defining what 'quality' education consists in, and by what and whose criteria of assessment.

Assessment

Then we read that **'Teaching continues to be dogged by low expectations, a lack of subject knowledge, weak curriculum planning and poor assessment of pupils' learning. As a result, pupils apply little effort in their work and do not make good enough progress'**. This statement requires considerable paradigmatic unpacking. First, no convincing evidence is provided in the inspection report for these assertions; but more importantly, this statement itself derives from a learning paradigm that privileges proceduralist content over *the humanistic and the emotional experience* of learning (e.g. Salzberger-Wittenberg et al., 1999) and *the quality of the learning experience* (van Manen, 1986, 1991) – with 'filling buckets' clearly taking precedence over 'lighting fires', as the famous saying goes.

Bucket-filling – and then measuring in a high-stakes way whether or not you've successfully filled the buckets in the pre-decided ways – is the learning paradigm (ideology) that has captured mainstream learning for decades, and which has been ratcheted up yet more since, some years back (2010–14), Michael Gove was Education Secretary of State. Yet this is an approach to learning that fundamentally contradicts the whole ethos and paradigmatic worldview of the Steiner Waldorf curriculum (and other humanistic learning paradigms) – where nourishing and finessing *the joy of the learning experience* and *feeding the children's imagination* are seen as far more important than is the filling of children's minds with 'facts'.

Thus, if Ofsted's whole approach to assessing schools and their learning were to be underpinned by a Steiner Waldorf curricular ethos rather than by the current

Audit Culture-driven one, it's very possible that the kind of learning observed at Wynstones would achieve high praise in many ways, whilst the learning in at least some of the schools that Ofsted currently rates as 'outstanding' would be heavily penalised. This is not to say that the Wynstones curriculum and teaching couldn't be improved – schools can always improve, and this applies to Wynstones as it does to any other school. And there could well be ways *within* its Waldorf curricular paradigm that significant improvements could be made at Wynstones. But it is vital to emphasise that Ofsted's judgements, as demonstrated in this report, do not constitute some objective, universal standard of school assessment, but are relative and unavoidably subjective according to its own highly contestable approach to what constitutes 'good' teaching and learning.

Moreover and as remarked earlier, if there were any evidence in this inspection report that the inspectors had made even a cursory attempt to understand the Waldorf curriculum before inspecting the school, and had then couched their judgements possessing such an understanding bearing key curricular differences in mind, then its assessments would carry more substance and would deserve to be taken more seriously. But as they stand, the judgements made here cannot be taken as a fair and pedagogically informed viewpoint – and certainly not one that should be being deployed as the pretext for the draconian closing of a school with barely any notice.

We are then told of **'Leaders' proposed actions to improve teaching and assessment…, and [proposing] to strengthen the curriculum and implement a new framework for assessing pupils'**. And so it is of little surprise that **'Most middle leaders have stepped away from their roles…'**.

What appears to have happened here is that the school co-principals ('leaders' in Ofsted's parlance) have uncritically complied with Ofsted's earlier demands about Wynstones' learning environment, which has in turn led to the understandable 'resistance' (discussed earlier) of many of the school's teachers to what was being demanded of them *that directly contradicted the Steiner Waldorf curriculum*, and so was perpetrating 'symbolic violence' (Bourdieu) on their professionalism as teachers (cf. Block, 2000). Based on a number of first-hand reports from teachers themselves, many of the teaching staff were also reacting to the non-collegial, non-collaborative methods employed by the co-principals – a phenomenon found in many settings where the recipients of quasi-authoritarian disciplinary measures (in this case, management from Ofsted) perpetrate the same methods on those whom they in turn oversee.

Next, the assertion that **'As a result, learning does not build on what pupils already know…'** is highly problematic. First, such a statement entails all manner of highly contestable assumptions about knowledge and our – and inspectors' – access to it. It presupposes that it is possible, in principle and in practice, to measure what children know in a proceduralist, conscious way. Yet as soon as one factors in 'the Unconscious' and psychodynamic aspects of learning (cited earlier), this assumption immediately collapses, as it is effectively assuming that only that which can be seen and measured exists and has pedagogical importance. I referred to the crucial issue of the psychodynamics of learning earlier in this counter-report (p. 74) as the failure to consider it is one of the most significant lacunae in Ofsted's whole approach to teaching and learning in England's schools.

At worst, then, what we are seeing here is an essentially robotic, formulaic assertion from within Ofsted's Audit Culture-informed 'regime of truth', that is making all manner of highly contestable assumptions about children's learning process that are entrenched within one particular paradigm – and is assuming that its own worldview (Kuhn, 1962) is necessarily the correct one, and that others are therefore wrong.

It is important to emphasise that this is emphatically not some kind of point-scoring exercise: I am not trying to score points in some 'battle of the egos'. Rather, I am pointing out that many if not most of the judgements on which Ofsted has based its fateful criticisms of Wynstones School are based on, and derive from, what are highly contestable and arguably fallacious assumptions. And to the extent that I succeed in making this argument, it follows logically that the forced closure of the school based on the pretexts given by Ofsted in their inspection report has no justification.

Next, we read that **'Reading is poorly taught and promoted…. Teachers do not know how to teach phonics'**. Again, we see a major clash of potentially incompatible pedagogical ideologies and practices here, about which the inspectors seem to have little if any awareness. Thus, in the realm of reading there exist different theories of learning, and the DfE/Ofsted are pushing just one of them – synthetic phonics – to the exclusion of others. It is not only within the Steiner Waldorf world where the imposition of synthetic phonics is seen as highly problematic (see, for example, Clark, 2014, 2016, 2018; Clark et al., 2016; Wyse, 2000; Wyse & Goswami, 2008; Wyse et al., 2018); and for many it is an unacceptably 'technocratic' and quasi-authoritarian intrusion into pedagogical professionalism for the DfE and Ofsted to be insisting upon reading being taught in one preferred way in all schools.

Moreover, there is an extensive and authoritative literature on the Waldorf approach to literacy (e.g. Allanson & Teensma, 2018), which has been developed from nearly a century of evolving teaching practice – an approach which crucially considers not only the crude measurable mechanics of reading competency and 'outcomes' beloved of Ofsted and the DfE, but which also considers the *developmental appropriateness* of reading as an activity in relation to the development of the child's developing consciousness, that needs to be introduced in a gradual and artistic, living way that is at the heart of Waldorf pedagogy.

There is also a substantial academic literature, led by Professor Sebastian Suggate in Germany, which shows conclusively that delaying the introduction of reading until age 7 not only does not hamper children's literacy development, but by the age of 11 or 12, such 'late starters' have not only caught up the early starters, but their love of and engagement in reading are at a significantly higher level of interest and commitment than that of early starters (Suggate 2009, 2011, 2012).

Furthermore, the statement that **'…a lack of books to support pupils' development of reading skills… puts pupils at this school at a significant disadvantage compared to others'** is again failing to recognise and acknowledge the major differences that exist between mainstream and Steiner Waldorf approaches to literacy development. Are the inspectors aware of these differences, and have they satisfied themselves that *within the specifically Waldorf approach* to literacy development, there is 'a lack of books'?

We read that **'Assessment strategies have been introduced in the lower school. However, there is no oversight of this.'** Another way of casting this statement would be to say that 'the level of enforcing compliance-cum-surveillance in the school wasn't good enough to ensure that compliance was total'. As I have emphasised elsewhere in this counter-report, of course teachers' compliance was at best half-hearted, because many if not most genuine Waldorf teachers faithful to their pedagogy, including those at Wynstones, see this as an attack on the integrity of the Steiner Waldorf curriculum – a curriculum which has a proud and distinguished history of a very light touch when it comes to testing, assessment, surveillance and all the other paraphernalia of the accountability-preoccupied Audit Culture (Monahan & Torres, 2009).

So when we read that **'Ongoing assessment of pupils' learning is weak at best and absent at worst'**, this criticism must be seen in the context of a tried-and-tested Waldorf curriculum that quite deliberately downplays assessment, for informed and carefully thought-through pedagogical reasons. Not least, it is a highly challengeable assumption that it is always necessary and appropriate that teachers should **'assess pupils' work'** – yet this appears to be an unquestioned normative assumption that Ofsted uncritically adopts and imposes without any critical reflection on the ideological position, and its effects, from which such a contestable assumption is being made.

Furthermore, Ofsted adopts a narrow view of assessment, referring exclusively to standardised and formal assessment. Yet all good teachers – and certainly Steiner Waldorf ones – are constantly 'assessing' children in order to best respond to their unique needs, ranging from a child's demeanour, interest and behaviour to her/his academic needs. The *whole child* is taken into consideration by the teacher, and informs their pedagogy. It would be procedurally impossible to formulate much of this into a quantitative 'assessment grid', such as Ofsted expects, demonstrating clear attainment progression; but that does not make it any less valid, and it is vital in supporting the development of the children in teachers' care. To assume that, in the absence of assessment grids, the teacher is not evaluating the best course for the pupils verges on being insulting to the teacher's professionalism.

So for Ofsted to first be uncritically imposing a univeralising Audit Culture ideology on to a Steiner school in this way, and then to be making negative judgements about that school when it doesn't tick their Audit Culture boxes and associated practices, is completely unacceptable from a Steiner Waldorf perspective – and particularly so when it appears that the inspectors seem to have no awareness of these core and strongly held philosophical-pedagogical divergences and incommensurabilities.

Having shown where the judgements in those parts of the inspection report dealing with issues other than safeguarding are questionable, I now move on in Chapter 4 to a wider discussion of the incommensurabilies between Ofsted's approach and that of humanistic Steiner Waldorf pedagogy, and how such divergences can be responded to.

PART III

Incommensurable Learning Paradigms – What Is To Be Done?

Chapter 4

Discussion

The first step on the road to wisdom is to reframe the whole idea of risk. We can dwell forever on worst-case scenarios…. But that's simply the wrong starting point.

TIM GILL

The overwhelming conclusion arising from the detailed critical analysis in the foregoing two chapters is that Ofsted's most recent inspection report on Wynstones School is littered with all manner of draconian and condemnatory judgements that are themselves founded in highly challengeable assumptions about child development and learning, and what constitutes appropriate teaching and pedagogical practice. Moreover, there is no evidence in the report to show that the inspectors have made any attempt to engage with understanding the differences between mainstream and Steiner Waldorf pedagogy, and then to reach nuanced judgements and assessments that take account of these philosophical and pedagogical divergences.

The decision to close Wynstones School based on condemnatory safeguarding judgements, which are seemingly founded on technical-procedural grounds rather than on the basis of actual serious incidents, is demonstrably disproportionate – and particularly in light of the very real safeguarding issues that have arisen directly from over 250 pupils being unexpectedly without a school from one day to the next, with some suffering from anxiety, depression and panic attacks, and older pupils' careers having been adversely affected (see the appendix to this book). As the foregoing painstaking line-by-line analysis of its inspection report has demonstrated, Ofsted's rationale for many if not most of its judgements of the school is at best problematic, and at worst, just plain wrong. The decision precipitately to close the school cannot therefore be justified.

The sensationalising local press reports on the Wynstones' forced closure were entirely predictable – namely, 'Pupils were "at significant risk of harm" at "toxic" Wynstones School' (13 February 2020); 'Wynstones School closes following damning Ofsted report' (28 January 2020); and most appalling of all – 'Kindergarten children were "at significant risk of harm" at "toxic" Wynstones Steiner School' (12 February) – with the press reporting verbatim and uncritically from what this counter-report has demonstrated to be the flawed Ofsted inspection report which precipitated the forced closure of the school.

It is unacceptable that a questionable inspection report should have been deployed as the pretext for forcibly closing a school in an action that has traumatised large numbers of children and families, and when the Department for Education will have known only too well what the inevitable consequences would be of their action.

We have it on legal authority that the evidence and the arguments presented in this counter-report, when taken alongside previous public statements made in correspondence between Ofsted's Amanda Spielman and the Secretary of State for Education (referred to earlier), make it distinctly possible that legal action taken against this treatment of Wynstones School will succeed in the law courts. It is my contention that Ofsted and the Department for Education are responsible for the unnecessary and unjustifiable ill-treatment of over 250 children and their families, and for this they must be held to account.

I am emphatically not claiming that there were no problems with Wynstones school, or that there were, and are, no areas where significant improvements could not be made. But what Ofsted and its inspectors need to demonstrate beyond reasonable doubt is that the shortcomings in the school were of such import and extent that they warranted the draconian step of precipitately closing the school, and leaving over 250 children to their families' own educational devices – many of them in the throes of preparing for potentially life-changing public examinations well before the current virus pandemic started. I maintain that my detailed analysis in this report of the pretexts given by inspectors for closing the school conclusively demonstrate that such a case was not adequately made in the case of this inspection and its inadequate report.

It seems clear that the Ofsted inspectors (whether deliberately, or as a function of being uncritically immersed in Ofsted's 'regime of truth' – or both) imported an inflexible, tick-box mentality that rigidly pre-defines what a 'good' school should look like; and when what they found at Wynstones did not coincide with their pre-decided template, they ipso facto assumed that the school was 'inadequate'(cf. Saville Kushner's Foreword). Again, this is a parody of what a fair and proportionate, *thoughtful* school inspection should be like, and it drives a coach and horses through any definition of natural justice. It is difficult not to construe the use of such a parody as the pretext for forcibly closing a school – against the wishes of the vast majority of happy children and satisfied parents – as anything less than a democratic outrage, which rides rough-shod over the human rights of parents to choose the education of their choice for their own children.

The arguments developed in this counter-report cannot *prove* with total certainty that Ofsted's inspection report on Wynstones Schools is wrong. I do have my own strong views on this question – but this is not at all the purpose of the above discussion. Rather, what this counter-report does demonstrate beyond reasonable doubt is that there exist very powerful, informed arguments that challenge much of the ideological substrate and associated practices that Ofsted demands of schools and teachers in its assessments of them. I further contend that Ofsted as an organisation, and certainly all of its inspectors, should be very aware of this issue, and that there exist teachers, schools and whole educational approaches which take fundamental issue with Ofsted's whole approach to Health, Safety and Safeguarding Culture and other key issues associated with the Audit Culture. As already quoted, in January 2019, head of Ofsted Amanda Spielman wrote to the then Education Secretary that 'there is a wide variety of educational philosophies, and successful schools can be run in a variety of ways. *Ofsted does not have a preferred model*' (my italics). I don't see any evidence to support this claim in the Ofsted inspection report on Wynstones Steiner School – and I see copious evidence that contradicts it.

It could conceivably be argued that, notwithstanding the wealth of evidence pointing to what Devine calls 'the adverse consequences of England's approach [to safeguarding] (2018, p. 2), in practice statutory agencies like Ofsted and schools have no choice but to interpret England's current legislation on safeguarding in a totally inflexible, procedural way. I am not a legal expert, and so am not qualified to comment on this key point. But what seems clear is that if, legally speaking, there does exist no latitude in the system for considered and proportionate professional judgement and flexibility to be exercised by dedicated professionals in school communities, then the law is a demonstrable ass – with the public–private balance having shifted much too far towards State intrusion (Devine, 2018) – and needs to be urgently re-visited to ensure that the kind of outrage to which Wynstones School and its devastated families and teachers have been subjected is never repeated.

In this counter-report, I have joined a long history of educationalists who have argued for many years that Ofsted's narrow Audit Culture mentality 'fetishises' the measurable and the procedural, and that as a result, its whole approach and mind-set seem incapable of doing other than a kind of (symbolic) violence to the tacit (van Manen, 1991), and to any learning experience that does not submit to, and comply with, its Audit Culture imperatives (e.g. House, 2000, 2002; cf. Bourdieu's conception of 'symbolic violence' – Bourdieu, 1992; Jenkins, 2002; Emmerich et al., 2015). Or as humanistic psychologist Abraham Maslow evocatively put it, 'When my only tool is a hammer, the world becomes a nail'.

When Strathern (2000b) wrote of the 'tyranny of transparency' at the turn of the century, she was making an essential point, which that other eminent global authority on the Audit Culture, Michael Power, also recognises: for

> the story of operational risk characterises a new risk management in which the imperative is to make visible and manageable *essentially unknowable and incalculable risks*.… [T]he cultural biases that drive the new risk management demand a procedural and auditable set of practices because *control must be made increasingly publicly visible* and because *organisational responsibility must be made transparent*. (Power, 2004, pp. 30, 41, my italics)

The implications of this highly 'inconvenient truth' for Audit Culture ideology and practices – that we can by no means assume that everything can be made transparent and auditable, and that the demand to do so is a historically located cultural artefact – can hardly be overestimated.

Finally, a brief but vital excursion into 'the psychoanalysis of organisations'. In any refounded accountability system for England's schools that moved beyond what I call the compliance-demanding 'Ofsted Enforcer' approach, the role and influence of *anxiety and its management in institutions* would be essential to address. Earlier in this book, I bemoaned the seeming lack of any awareness of the *psychodynamics* of learning, teaching and relationships in Ofsted's understandings of, and judgements about, schools. There exists a substantial literature on the *unconscious psychological dynamics* that obtain in hospitals and medical settings, stemming from important pioneering work carried out by Isabel Menzies Lyth and Eliott Jaques many decades ago on the phenomenon of *anxiety in institutions*, and how it gets (or doesn't get) contained and managed, commonly in highly dysfunctional ways.

In brief, Menzies-Lyth (or Menzies, as she was then) was asked by senior hospital staff to help improve the method of allocating student nurses to practical (non-classroom) work. As her data collection proceeded, her attention was repeatedly drawn towards the considerable levels of anxiety and distress that she observed amongst the nurses. She made theoretical sense of this phenomenon by drawing upon the psychoanalytic ideas of Melanie Klein and Elliott Jaques (see Jaques, 1955; Menzies Lyth, 1988; Long, 2006; and Lawlor, 2009), with Klein arguing that when under stress, adults can easily regress to 'splitting' and projecting so-called 'bad objects' outside of themselves. Jaques then built on Klein's ideas, viewing events in organisations in the context of social systems which, he argued, tend to develop (out of people's conscious awareness) as *a defence against persecutory anxiety*.

Thus, Menzies-Lyth discovered how collective defences had become unconsciously institutionalised in working practices and in the social system – seeing strong parallels between the objective situation facing nurses in their working environment, and the unconscious 'phantasies' that exist in the most primitive levels of the mind. The kinds of techniques she identified that were deployed in order to contain the anxiety within the nursing service were 'depersonalisation and denial of significance of the individual', 'detachment and denial of feelings' and 'the attempt to eliminate decisions by ritual task-performance'.

Not only did these various techniques only contribute very marginally to reducing anxiety, but *secondary* anxieties were generated, which themselves created further defences in the organisation. I hope it will be clear from this all-too-brief foray into institutions, and the ways in which they function in relation to unprocessed anxiety, that there is a rich potential for insight from these ideas in terms of the way that schools function when subjected to the high-stakes accountability regime of which Ofsted is the enforcer. I hope my point will be obvious: first, that Ofsted's very existence, with its well known 'enforcer' approach, generates massive amounts of conscious *and unconscious* anxiety in schools, which will in turn have comparably massive impacts on a school's functioning, at both individual and structural/institutional levels; and secondly, that if inspectors are not aware of these toxic psychodynamics and their effects, they are very likely to be chronically misspecifying the nature of the 'problems' they discover in the schools they inspect.

From my knowledge of Wynstones School, it seems unarguable that the degree of anxiety and fear generated in the school by Ofsted's whole approach had enormous impacts on the school's functioning.

CHAPTER 5

Conclusion

[W]hat is the appropriate balance between the powers of the State and the private rights of citizens, including children, to question and prevent unwanted or unwarranted intrusion and interference?

LAUREN DEVINE

Michael Power's notion of 'the risk management of everything' (Power, 2004), referred to earlier, is highly illuminating regarding the safeguarding ideology that has grown like flotsam in England since the 1990s (Broadhurst et al., 2009a), and the uncritical enforcement of which Ofsted takes so seriously. Yet for Power,

> the primary driver of the risk management of everything *has nothing to do with organisational efficiency*, although it will be marketed in this way. Rather, it arises from *the increasingly defensive mood of agents who previously absorbed risk on behalf of others*. These risk management agents – e.g. teachers… and anyone else exercising a judgement on behalf of others – have become preoccupied with their own risks. Coupled to institutionalised assumptions and myths about the manageability of risks, *there is an intensification of strategies to avoid blame* when things go wrong…. The result is a *potentially catastrophic downward spiral in which expert judgement shrinks to an empty form of defendable compliance.* (p. 42, my italics)

These are crucial insights, the intricacies, depth and full implications of which cannot be pursued in this short book. But they do point to the fact that safeguarding ideology and its associated practices constitute a field of great organisational, psychological and cultural-historical complexity which render it singularly inappropriate for applying simplistic Audit Culture metrics and 'blame and shame' punishment practices in order to 'deliver' it. I would certainly want to claim that what has happened with Wynstones School is a paradigm case of what Power terms the 'catastrophic downward spiral in which expert judgement shrinks to an empty form of defendable compliance'.

With more specific reference to the circumstances carefully outlined in this book, I maintain that **Ofsted has a grave responsibility to take principled ideological differences fully into account in the decisions, demands and judgements it makes** – not least around the vexed issue of safeguarding. And in the case of the precipitate, arguably brutal decision to close Wynstones Steiner school virtually overnight, Ofsted and the Department for Education have signally failed in this professional duty – and at worst, they have put the enforcing of 'Ofsted-knows-best' compliance before a sensible, open-minded engagement with an educational philosophy which is not only very different from its own worldview –

but from which it might actually have a great deal to learn, if only it were open to such learning (Woods et al., 2005).

Ofsted and the Department for Education have a stark choice. They can engage open-mindedly with the arguments in this counter-report, and demonstrate a genuine openness to looking self-critically and constructively at their own ideology and associated practices in order to improve them – which will include locating their own organisation and approach within a wider cultural/paradigmatic perspective (Creasy, 2020); or they can baton down the hatches, and either ignore this counter-report and its detailed arguments, or actively discredit it. The way in which they do – or do not – respond will show whether Ofsted is an organisation that is equipped with the post-authoritarian flexibility, humility and reflexivity to deserve to be evaluating England's schools in the twenty-first century.

It's not as if there don't exist viable, far more human alternatives to the Ofsted approach dissected in detail in this counter-report. As described by Saville Kushner in the Foreword to this book, it is by no means impossible to organise and implement what Power terms 'soft management systems' in relation to school accountability, as opposed to the hard, compliance-inculcating and punishment-oriented Ofsted approach. As Power writes,

> The policy and managerial challenge is to attenuate and dampen the tendency for control systems to provide layers of pseudo-comfort about risk. There is a need to design soft management systems *capable of addressing uncomfortable uncertainties and deep-seated working assumptions*, overcoming the psychological and institutional need to fit recalcitrant phenomena into well tried, incrementally adjusted, linear frameworks of understanding. (Power, 2004, pp. 50–1, my italics)

And later, Power writes of 'developing a public language of risk that explicitly admits the possibility of failure' (p. 58), with 'myths of perfect Manageability… laid to rest, but [with] necessarily imperfect, humanly designed and operated, risk management systems continu[ing] to support an engagement with unknowable futures' (ibid.); 'an intelligent risk management [that] would not allow control systems, and their advocates, to swamp managerial attention and *independent critical imagination*' (p. 61. my italics); 'Risk management would be characterised more by learning and experiment, rather than rule-based processes' (ibid.); 'the new politics of uncertainty must generate legitimacy for the possibility of failure' (p. 62); 'A new politics of uncertainty would not seek to assuage public anxiety and concerns with images and rhetorics of manageability and control, and would challenge assumptions that all risk is manageable' (p. 63); 'the test of good governance would not necessarily be the speed of their reaction to failure; on the contrary, it might be their ability, in Peter Senge's phrase, "to take two aspirin and wait" (ibid.); and perhaps most crucially:

> a new politics of uncertainty must provide the necessary, if not sufficient, institutional conditions, for intelligent trust in expert judgement to flourish, and for the recovery and development of the idea of *honest professional opinion*. We need to imagine and create *'safe havens' for professional and expert judgement*. These havens would be safe in the sense of providing a space for decision-making where competence may flourish and express itself. (ibid., my italics)

And at the very end of his essay:

> If we must act as if we know the risks we face, then we must also create forms of risk management, and a related politics of uncertainty, which allows us to do this in more, rather than less, intelligent ways. (p. 65)

A careful reading of Power, and of existing successful school accountability alternatives around the world, gives the lie to the unsustainable view that there is no alternative to Ofsted's way.

Let me finish this book with the most charitable complexion I can place on the distressing events described herein. It is just possible that everything that has happened in this deeply distressing saga can be accounted for by the existence of what are fundamentally incommensurable and incompatible educational worldviews, which are so different from one another that Ofsted as an organisation is not able to understand an approach to learning and education – humanistic Steiner Waldorf education – which rejects many of Ofsted's and the Audit Culture's core assumptions. And further, that it is this lack of understanding that has generated the current malaise, and has led Ofsted (and possibly the Department for Education) to judge as 'inadequate' a pedagogical system that does not fall in sufficiently with its own ideology – thence leading to a school being forced to close against the will of the vast majority of children and parents associated with that school.

Others will have to judge whether this latter explanation accounts for what has happened in its entirety, or whether other forces have also been operating. At present as I write, I retain an open mind on these questions; and a deep conversation with Ofsted – possibly in the law courts – might be the only way to resolve these grave matters; for they are issues that call into severe question the very raison d'être and bona fides of Ofsted as the institution responsible for holding our schools to account.

To repeat, in closing this counter-report and book: on any dispassionate view of the evidence, I maintain that Ofsted and the Department for Education are effectively responsible for the unnecessary abuse and traumatisation of over 250 children and their families through the forced, unjustifiable closing of their school. In the case of Ofsted, it is long overdue that *accountability itself* needs to be held robustly to account (Sirotnik, 2004) – and the case made in this book should very much be seen in this principled context.

Richard House, MA (Oxon), Ph.D., C.Psychol., AFBPsS, Cert.Couns.
Registered Chartered Psychologist (BPS) and Independent Educational Consultant
Stroud, Gloucestershire
March 2020

References

Allanson, A. & Teensma, N. (2018). *Writing to Reading the Steiner Waldorf Way: Foundations of Creative Literacy in Classes 1 and 2*. Stroud, Gloucestershire: Hawthorn Press.

Apple, M.W. (2004). Schooling, markets, and an audit culture. *Educational Policy*, 18 (4): 614–21.

Apple, M.W. (2005a). Education, markets, and an audit culture. *Critical Quarterly*, 47 (1–2): 11–29.

Apple, M.W. (2005b). Audit cultures, commodification, and class and race strategies in education. *Policy Futures in Education*, 3 (4): 379–99.

Arthur, J. (2015). Extremism and neo-liberal education policy: a contextual critique of the Trojan Horse Affair in Birmingham schools. *British Journal of Educational Studies*, 63 (3): 311–28.

Atkinson, T. & Claxton, G. (2000a). Introduction. In T. Atkinson & G. Claxton (eds), *The Intuitive Practitioner: On the Value of Not Always Knowing what One Is Doing* (pp. 1–11). Buckingham: Open University Press.

Atkinson, T. & Claxton, G. (eds) (2000b). *The Intuitive Practitioner: On the Value of Not Always Knowing what One Is Doing*. Buckingham: Open University Press.

Betti, M. (2019). *Twelve Ways of Seeing the World: Philosophies and Archetypal Worldviews for Understanding Human Consciousness*. Stroud, Gloucestershire: Hawthorn Press.

Blair, T. (2002). *The Courage of Our Convictions*. London: Fabian Society.

Block, A.A. (2000). *I'm Only Bleeding: Education as the Practice of Social Violence against Children*, 2nd edn. New York: Peter Lang.

Bortoft, H. (1996). *The Wholeness of Nature: Goethe's Way of Science*. Edinburgh: Floris Books.

Bourdieu, P. (1992). *Language and Symbolic Power*. Cambridge: Polity Press.

Brinton, R. (2020). Ofsted seeks judgement-free approach to 'stuck schools' – but what about its own 'stuck' methods of accountability? *Association for Humanistic Psychology Magazine for Self & Society*, no. 4 (Winter); available at https://tinyurl.com/snbxr32 (accessed 18 February 2020).

Brinton, R. & Glöckler, M. (eds) (2019). *Growing up Healthy in a World of Digital Media: A Guide for Parents and Caregivers of Children and Adolescents*. Stroud, Gloucestershire: InterActions.

Broadhurst, K., Grover, C., & Jamieson, J. (eds) (2009a). *Critical Perspectives on Safeguarding Children*. Chichester, West Sussex: Wiley.

Broadhurst, K., Grover, C., & Jamieson, J. (2009b). Introduction: safeguarding children? In their *Critical Perspectives on Safeguarding Children* (pp. 1–16). Chichester, West Sussex: Wiley.

Brown, T. & Hanlon, M. (2014). *Playing by the Rules: How Our Obsession with Safety Is Putting Us All at Risk*. London: Sphere.

Buckingham, D. (2000). *After the Death of Childhood: Growing Up in the Age of Electronic Media*. Cambridge: Polity.

Burchell, S. (2019–2020). Sick of safeguarding. *Association for Humanistic Psychology Magazine for Self & Society*, no. 4 (Winter); available at https://tinyurl.com/u45fkf5 (accessed 20 February 2020).

Carey, M. (2008). Everything must go? The privatization of State social work. *British Journal of Social Work*, 38: 918–35.

Carnie, F., Large, M., & Tasker, M. (eds) (1995). *Freeing Education: Steps towards Real Choice and Diversity in Schools*. Stroud, Gloucestershire: Hawthorn Press.

Clark, M.M. (2014). *Synthetic Phonics and Literacy Learning: An Evidence-Based Critique*. Birmingham: Glendale Education.

Clark, M.M. (2016). *Learning To Be Literate: Insights from Research for Policy and Practice*.

Abingdon, Oxon: Routledge.

Clark, M.M. (ed.) (2018). *Teaching Initial Literacy: Policies, Evidence and Ideology*. Birmingham: Glendale Education.

Clark, M.M. & 6 others (2016). *Reading the Evidence: Synthetic Phonics and Literacy Learning*. Birmingham: Glendale Education.

Clarke-Wellsmore, D. (2017). A cure worse than the disease: the data-surveillance approach to child protection. 28 November; available at tremr.com/deccw/a-cure-worse-than-the-disease-the-data-surveillance-approach-to-child-protection (accessed 12 March 2020).

Claxton, G. (1997a). *Hare Brain, Tortoise Mind: Why Intelligence Increases when You Think Less*. London: Fourth Estate.

Claxton, G. (1997b). Premature articulation: how thinking gets in the way of learning. In his *Hare Brain, Tortoise Mind: Why Intelligence Increases when You Think Less* (pp. 28–47). London: Fourth Estate.

Claxton, G. (1997c). Perception without consciousness. In his *Hare Brain, Tortoise Mind: Why Intelligence Increases when You Think Less* (pp. 100–15). London: Fourth Estate.

Cooper, A. Katz, I., & Hetherington, R. (2003). *The Risk Factor*. London: Demos; available at https://tinyurl.com/ua9427x (accessed 12 March 2020).

Creasy, R. (2020). *Resilience, Risk and Safeguarding: A Critical Introduction for Childhood Studies*. Indep. publ.

Creasy, R. & Corby, F. (2019). *Taming Childhood?: A Critical Perspective on Policy, Practice and Parenting*. Basingstoke: Palgrave Macmillan.

Davou, B. (2002). Unconscious processes influencing learning. *Psychodynamic Practice*, 8 (3): 277–94.

Devine, L. (2018). *The Limits of State Power and Private Rights: Exploring Child Protection and Safeguarding Referrals and Assessments*. Abingdon, Oxon: Routledge.

Devine, L. & Parker, S. (2015). *Rethinking Child Protection Strategy: Learning from Trends*. Bristol: Working Paper, Centre for Legal Research, Bristol Law School, UWE / Economic and Social Research Council, March; available at https://tinyurl.com/s8thbcl (accessed 10 March 2020).

Douglas, M. & Wildavsky, A. (1983). *Risk and Culture*. Berkeley: University of California Press.

Dover, J. (2002). The child who cannot bear being taught. *Psychodynamic Practice*, 8 (3): 311–25.

Emmerich, N., Swinglehurst, D., Maybin, J. & others (2015). Caring for quality of care: symbolic violence and the bureaucracies of audit. *BMC Medical Ethics*, 16, 23; available at https://tinyurl.com/r9uqcz4 (retrieved 22 February 2020).

Featherstone, B., Broadhurst, K., & Holt, K. (2012). Thinking systemically – thinking politically: building strong partnerships with children and families in the context of rising inequality. *British Journal of Social Work*, 42: 618–33.

Furedi, F. (1997). *The Culture of Fear: Risk Taking and the Morality of Low Expectations*. London: Cassell.

Furedi, F, (2018). *How Fear Works: Culture of Fear in the 21st Century*. London: Bloomsbury Continuum.

Furedi, F. & Bristow, J. (2008). *Licensed to Hug: How Child Protection Policies Are Poisoning the Relationship Between the Generations and Damaging the Voluntary Sector*. London: Civitas.

Gill, T. (2007). *No Fear: Growing up in a Risk Averse Society*. London: Calouste Gulbenkian Foundation.

Goleman, D. (1996). *Emotional Intelligence: Why It Can Matter More Than IQ*. London: Bloomsbury.

Greenfield, S. (2018–9). The use of digital technology and the health and wellbeing of children and young people. *Association for Humanistic Psychology Magazine for*

Self & Society, 2 (Winter); available at https://tinyurl.com/rj28ter (accessed 12 March 2020).

Hall, J. (1993). *The Reluctant Adult: An Exploration of Choice.* Bridport, Dorset: Prism Press.

Hanko, G. (2002). Making psychodynamic insights accessible to teachers as an integral part of their professional task. *Psychodynamic Practice*, 8 (3): 375–89.

HM Government (2006). *Working Together to Safeguard Children: A Guide to Inter-Agency Working to Safeguard and Promote the Welfare of Children.* London: Stationery Office.

House, R. (1997). Participatory ethics in a self-generating practitioner community. In R. House & N. Totton (eds), *Implausible Professions: Arguments for Pluralism and Autonomy in Psychotherapy and Counselling* (pp. 321–34). Ross-on-Wye: PCCS Books.

House, R. (2000). Stress, surveillance and modernity: the 'modernising' assault on our education system. *Education Now*, 30 (Winter), Special supplement (4 pp).

House, R. (2002). '…A sort of professional rape': exposing the violations of 'modernised' education. *Education Now*, 35 (Spring)

House, R. (2003–4). Beyond 'paranoid parenting': raising children in a fear-filled age. *The Mother* magazine, 8 (Winter): 6–9.

House, R. (ed.) (2011). *Too Much, Too Soon? Early Learning and the Erosion of Childhood.* Stroud, Gloucestershire: Hawthorn Press.

House, R. (2014). 'Principled Non-compliance': an idea whose time has come? *Nursery World*, 23 April; available at https://tinyurl.com/sshh84o (accessed 20 February 2020).

House, R. (2017). Beyond the measurable: alternatives to managed care in research and practice. In J. Lees (ed.), *The Future of the Psychological Therapies* (pp. 148–66). Abingdon, Oxon: Routledge.

House, R. (2018a). 'Principled non-compliance': some background to a new cultural movement. *Association for Humanistic Psychology Magazine for Self & Society*, no. 1, Winter; available at https://tinyurl.com/qktlwbj (accessed 18 February 2020; available from the author on request); see also House, 2014.

House, R. (2018b). Education beyond capital and the neoliberal state: challenging the 'academizing' of England's schools. In M. Large & S. Briault (eds), *Free, Mutual and Equal: Rebalancing Society for the Common Good* (pp. 194–210). Stroud, Gloucestershire: Hawthorn Press.

Jack, G. (1997). Discourses of child protection and child welfare. *British Journal of Social Work*, 27: 659–78.

Jaques, E. (1955). Social systems as a defence against persecutory and depressive anxiety. In M. Klein, P. Heimann & R.E. Money-Kyrle (eds), *New Directions in Psycho-Analysis* (pp. 478–98). London: Tavistock Publications.

Jeffrey, B. & Woods, P. (1996). Feeling deprofessionalised: the social construction of emotions during an OFSTED inspection. *Cambridge Journal of Education*, 26 (3): 325–43.

Jenkins, R. (2002). *Pierre Bourdieu*, 2nd edn. London: Routledge.

Karpman, S.B. (2004). *A Game Free Life: The Definitive Book on the Drama Triangle and Compassion Triangle by the Originator and Author.* San Francisco, Calif.: Drama Triangle Publications.

Kerr, P. (2017). High Court finds OFSTED's complaints procedure 'unfair'. Tees Law, 23 August; available at https://tinyurl.com/u55ptp7 (accessed 15 March 2020).

Kuhn, T.S. (1962). *The Structure of Scientific Revolutions.* Chicago: Chicago University Press.

Large, M. & Briault, S. (eds) (2018). *Free, Mutual and Equal: Rebalancing Society for the Common Good.* Stroud, Gloucestershire: Hawthorn Press.

Lawlor, D. (2009). A case study in the functioning of social systems as a defence against anxiety: rereading 50 years on. *Clinical and Child Psychology and Psychiatry*, 14 (4): 523–30.

Long, S. (2006). Organizational defences against anxiety: what has happened since the 1955 Jaques paper? *International Journal of Applied Psychoanalytic Studies*, 3 (4): 279–95.

McGillivray, A. (1997). Governing childhood. In A. McGillivray (ed.), *Governing Childhood* (pp. 1–24). Aldershot: Dartmouth Publ. Co.

Mayes, C. (2009). The psychoanalytic view of teaching and learning, 1922–2002. *Journal of Curriculum Studies*, 41 (4): 539–67.

Menzies Lyth, I. (1988). *Containing Anxiety in Institutions: Selected Essays, Volume 1.* London: Free Association Books.

Monahan, T. & Torres, R.D. (2009). *Schools under Surveillance: Cultures of Control in Public Education.* New Brunswick, NJ: Rutgers University Press.

Naydler, J. (1996). *Goethe on Science: An Anthology of Goethe's Scientific Writing.* Edinburgh: Floris Books.

Neville, B. (1989). *Educating Psyche: Emotion, Imagination and the Unconscious in Learning.* North Blackburn, Victoria, Austr.: Collins Dove/Harper.

Office for Standards in Education (Ofsted) (2018). *Complaints about Ofsted: Raising Concerns and Making a Complaint about Ofsted.* Manchester, May. Reference no: 170013; available at https://tinyurl.com/r6aaute (accessed 14 March 2020).

Office for Standards in Education (Ofsted) (2020). *Fight or Flight? How 'Stuck' Schools Are Overcoming Isolation: Evaluation Report:* Manchester: Office for Standards in Education (Ofsted); available at https://tinyurl.com/vytegmt (accessed 25 February 2020).

Page, D. (2017). Conceptualising the surveillance of teachers. *British Journal of Sociology of Education*, 38 (7): 991–1006.

Palmer, S. (2015). *Toxic Childhood: How the Modern World Is Damaging Our Children and What We Can Do About It.* London: Orion Books.

Parton, N. (2006). *Safeguarding Childhood: Early Intervention and Surveillance in a Late Modern Society.* Basingstoke: Palgrave Macmillan.

Parton, N. (2010). Review of Broadhurst et al., 2009. *Critical Social Policy*, 30 (4): 592–4.

Postman, N. (1995). *The Disappearance of Childhood.* New York: Vintage.

Power, M. (1997). *The Audit Society: Rituals of Verification.* Oxford: Oxford University Press.

Power, M. (2004). *The Risk Management of Everything: Rethinking the Politics of Uncertainty.* London: DEMOS; available at https://tinyurl.com/ve5bvcm (accessed 8 March 2020).

Pring, R. (1995). Role of the state in education. In F. Carnie & others (eds), *Freeing Education* (pp. 3–9). Stroud, Gloucestershire: Hawthorn Press.

Reinsmith, W.A. (1989). The whole in every part: Steiner and Waldorf schooling. *Educational Forum*, 54 (1): 79–91.

Rivers, I. & Soutter, A. (1996). Bullying and the Steiner school ethos. *School Psychology International*, 17: 359–77.

Roberts, J. (2020). 'Basic errors': 6 complaints about Ofsted inspections. *Times Educational Supplement*, 14 February; available at https://tinyurl.com/sd59sfs (accessed 15 March 2020).

Robinson, M. (2016). Show or tell: how should educators and playworkers back up their real-time decisions about risk? – Tim Gill blog entry comment, 26 May. Available at https://tinyurl.com/vbewco2 (accessed 16 February 2020).

Rose, N. (1989). *Governing the Soul: The Shaping of the Private Self.* London: Routledge.

Sahlberg, P. (2014). *Finnish Lessons 2.0: What Can the World Learn from Educational Change in Finland?*, 2nd edn. New York: Teachers College Press / Columbia University.

Saltzman, C. (2006). Introducing teachers to a psychodynamically informed teaching practice. *Psychodynamic Practice*, 12 (1): 67–86.

Salzberger-Wittenberg, I., Williams, & Osborne, E. (1999). *The Emotional Experience of Learning and Teaching.* London: Karnac Books.

Schön, D.A. (1983), *The Reflective Practitioner: How Professionals Think in Action.* New

York: Basic Books.

Schön, D.A. (1987). *Educating the Reflective Practitioner: Toward a New Design for Teaching and Learning*. London: Jossey-Bass/Wiley.

Seamon, D. & Zajonc, A. (1998). *Goethe's Way of Science*. New York: State University of New York Press.

Senge, P. (2006). *The Fifth Discipline: The Art and Practice of the Learning Organization*, 2nd edn. New York and London: Random House.

Sirotnik, K.A. (ed.) (2004). *Holding Accountability Accountable: What Ought to Matter in Public Education*. Columbia University, New York: Teachers College Press.

Spielman, A. (2019). Correspondence: Steiner schools: Amanda Spielman writes to Damian Hinds, 31 January; available at https://tinyurl.com/ukud32s (accessed 14 March 2020).

Strathern, M. (ed.) (2000a). *Audit Cultures: Anthropological Studies in Accountability, Ethics and the Academy* (EASA series). London: Routledge.

Strathern, M. (2000b). The tyranny of transparency. *British Educational Research Journal*, 26: 309–21.

Suggate, S.P. (2009). School entry age and reading achievement in the 2006 Programme for International Student Assessment (PISA). *International Journal of Educational Research*, 48: 151–61.

Suggate, S.P. (2011). Viewing the long-term effects of early reading with an open eye. In R. House (ed.), *Too Much, Too Soon? Early Learning and the Erosion of Childhood* (pp. 236–46). Stroud, Gloucestershire: Hawthorn Press.

Suggate, S.P. (2012). Watering the garden before a rainstorm: the case of early reading. In S.P. Suggate & E. Reese (eds), *Contemporary Debates in Child Development and Education* (pp. 181–90). London: Routledge.

Wastell, D., White, S., Broadhurst, K., Peckover, S., & Pithouse, A. (2010). Children's services in the iron cage of performance management: street-level bureaucracy and the spectre of Švejkism. *International Journal of Social Welfare*, 19: 310–20.

Weinhold, B.K. & Weinhold, J.B. (2017). *How to Break Free of the Drama Triangle and Victim Consciousness*. Colorado Springs, Colo.: CICRCL Press.

van Manen, M. (1986). *The Tone of Teaching*. Richmond Hill, Ontario: TAB Publishers.

van Manen, M. (1991). *The Tact of Teaching: The Meaning of Pedagogical Thoughtfulness*. New York: State University of New York Press.

White, S. (2009). Arguing the case in safeguarding. In K. Broadhurst & others (eds), *Critical Perspectives on Safeguarding Children* (pp. 93–110). Chichester, West Sussex: Wiley.

Woods, P., Ashley, M., & Woods, G. (2005). *Steiner Schools in England*. Department for Education and Skills / University of West of England, Bristol; Research Report RR645; available at https://tinyurl.com/slv8yod (accessed 14 March 2020).

Wrennall, L. (2010). Surveillance and child protection: de-mystifying the Trojan horse. *Surveillance & Society*, 7 (3–4): 304–24; available at https://tinyurl.com/s4z7lmq (accessed 12 March 2020).

Wyse, D. (2000). Phonics – the whole story? A critical review of empirical evidence. *Educational Studies*, 26 (3): 355–64.

Wyse, D. & Goswami, U. (2008). Synthetic phonics and the teaching of reading. *British Educational Research Journal*, 34 (6): 691–710.

Wyse, D., Jones, R., Bradford, H. & Wolpert, M.A. (2018). *Teaching English, Language and Literacy*, 4th edn. Abingdon, Oxon: Routledge.

Young, M. (Lord) (1995). Foreword: *Go for diversity!* In F. Carnie & others (eds), *Freeing Education* (pp. vii–viii). Stroud, Gloucestershire: Hawthorn Press.

Zohar, D. & Marshall, I. (2001). *Spiritual Intelligence: The Ultimate Intelligence*. London: Bloomsbury.

Select Critical Bibliography on Ofsted

This is a highly select bibliography which contains only a small fraction of the extensive literature available that critiques the Ofsted regime, with more recent literature being given most prominence here.

Anon (2020). ASCL: Ofsted must do more to build faith in complaints system. 1 April; available at https://tinyurl.com/wpwpqwz; accessed 12 April 2020.

Avison, K. (2008). What does Ofsted inspect? A Steiner Waldorf perspective. In A. de Waal (ed.), *Inspecting the Inspectorate: Ofsted under Scrutiny* (pp. 96–105, 111–12). London: Civitas; available at https://tinyurl.com/ng2zdju (accessed 30 March 2020).

Bassey, M. & others (2020). Letters – An Ofsted inspection should not be like entering the dragons' den. The *Guardian*, 8 February; available at https://tinyurl.com/rvaz2qc (accessed 16 February 2020).

Bousted, M. (2020). Schools deserve better than an inspectorate that's come unstuck. Schools Week website, 9 January; available at https://tinyurl.com/ws6hkmh (accessed 4 February 2020).

Bousted, M. & Wrigley, P. (2020). Ofsted casts a dark shadow over schools – letters. The *Guardian*, Wednesday 26 Februrary; available at https://tinyurl.com/uouoegk; accessed 27 February 2020.

Brinton, R. & House, R, (2019a). Talking Point: Richard Brinton and Richard House describe a new campaign for radically reforming or replacing Ofsted. *Juno* magazine, Autumn: 43.

Brinton, R. & House, R, (2019b). INSTED, not Ofsted…: A new campaign for a better nursery and schooling system and inspectorate is needed. *Nursery World*, 1 September; available at https://tinyurl.com/u23wpt5 (accessed 12 March 2020).

Case, P., Case, S., & Catling, S. (2000). Please show you're working: a critical assessment of the impact of OFSTED inspection on primary teachers. *British Journal of Sociology of Education*, 21 (4): 605–21.

CEPPP (1999). *The Ofsted System of School Inspection: An Independent Evaluation. Report of a Study*. Uxbridge: Centre for the Evaluation of Public Policy and Practice, Brunel University.

Coffield, F. (2017). *Will the Leopard Change Its Spots? A New Model of Inspection for Ofsted*. London: UCL Institute of Education Press.

Coffield, F. (2019). A world without Ofsted. *Times Educational Supplement* podcast; available at https://tinyurl.com/t4zy72y (accessed 1 April 2020).

Cullingford, C. (ed.) (1999). *An Inspector Calls: Ofsted and Its Effect on School Standards*. London: Kogan Page.

de Waal, A. (ed.) (2006). *Inspection, Inspection, Inspection! How Ofsted Crushes Independent Schools and Independent Teachers*. London: Civitas; available at https://tinyurl.com/toncpzr (accessed 30 March 2020).

de Waal, S. (ed.) (2008). *Inspecting the Inspectorate: Ofsted under Scrutiny*. London: Civitas; available at https://tinyurl.com/ng2zdju (accessed 30 March 2020).

Duffy, M. (ed.) (1996). *A Better System of Inspection: Report of Conference Proceedings at New College, Oxford, June 1996*. Hexam: Office for Standards in Inspection (OFSTIN).

Fairclough, M. (2020). If Ofsted told us to jump off a cliff, would we? *Times Educational Supplement*, 20 February; available at https://tinyurl.com/rxz985r (accessed 20 February 2020).

House, R. (2007). Schooling, the state and children's psychological well-being: a psychosocial critique. *Journal of Psychosocial Research* 2 (July–Dec): 49–62.

House, R. & Brinton, R. (2019), Time for something INSTED of Ofsted... *Early Years Educator*, 21 (6): 12.

House, R., Brinton, R., & 54 others (2019). An Open Letter to Amanda Spielman (Head of Ofsted), 25 June; available at https://tinyurl.com/y3x8f5k6 (accessed 4 February 2020).

Jeffrey, B. & Woods, P. (1996). Feeling deprofessionalised: the social construction of emotions during an OFSTED inspection. *Cambridge Journal of Education*, 26 (3): 325–43.

Reclaiming Schools (2020) (in press). *Ofsted beyond Repair: Alternatives for School Evaluation*. Book in press.

Schools Week reporter (2020). 8 January; available at https://tinyurl.com/rujkjfc (accessed 4 February 2020).

Thomas, B., Lowry, F., & Lewinski, M. (2017). Letters – Ofsted and the harm done by school league tables. The *Guardian*, 26 June; available at https://tinyurl.com/y8ku646l (accessed 4 February 2020).

Thomson, C. (2016). Ofsted is responsible for a culture of fear in schools that too often results in job losses. *Times Educational Supplement*, 5 October; available at https://tinyurl.com/sda3nhw (accessed 20 February 2020).

Tierney, S. (2020). Teachers are drowning in our pernicious Ofsted system. *Times Educational Supplement*, 11 March; available at https://tinyurl.com/qty55gc (accessed 12 March 2020).

Trafford, B. (2016). Ministers call it cracking down on poor performance. I call it persecution of a once noble and now beleaguered profession. *Times Educational Supplement*, 7 January; available at https://tinyurl.com/rf5twyh (accessed 12 March 2020)

APPENDIX

Wynstones Parents' Voices on the School Closure

Introduction

A simple questionnaire was sent to a number of Wynstones parents, inviting their comments on their and their children's experiences of the Wynstones School closure. The questionnaire was compiled and circulated in the spirit of genuine and open inquiry, as we wished to discover what the experience of the school's closing had been like for families. We were careful to ask for parents' positive as well as negative experiences of the closure, so in this sense the wording of the questionnaire was impeccably neutral.

Below is a full report of the responses that were received – over 30 in all. This is in no way a 'scientific', representative sample – in the circumstances in which this data were collected, there is no conceivable way in which it could be, as we had no way of contacting all parents in the school. However, what we present below is a report, with verbatim quotations, of the responses we received – and in that sense it provides important information about the impact of the closure on the parents who have responded. It makes for deeply distressing reading.

All but one respondent gave their express permission for their comments to be quoted verbatim – anonymously, of course (and disguised when someone's identity might be revealed by the quotation being used, e.g. by removing gendered statements about children; this makes for clumsy reading, but is essential to ensure confidentiality of the respondents).

The negative experiences reported in this survey dwarfed any positive ones – but in the spirit of balance, all of the substantive positive comments we did receive are reproduced in a sub-section below. This report, and subsequent updatings, is available at https://tinyurl.com/uqwxzjy. Note that the letter designation below simply refers to the order in which we received questionnaire responses.

Our thanks and appreciation to those parents who took the trouble to complete and return the questionnaire, and for having the courage to share what in many cases are deeply distressing experiences. Gratitude, and deep respect.

Richard House and Richard Brinton

Stroud, March 2020

SELECT GENERAL COMMENTS

… Words don't capture the impact the closure has had on our family. [A]

…we are reeling from the shock that the DfE has the power to shut down a school with no notice and no support. [A]

…Was the school so bad that Ofsted had to close it down immediately, with the knock-on impact that has had on families, children and communities – absolutely not! [A]

Our children were being held in a very safe and supporting space in Class xxxx. [A]

… It's reassuring to know that efforts are being made behind the scenes on our's and the school's behalf. [A]

…s/he still wants to go back to Wynstones. If s/he has even one friend left in her/his class, s/he says she wants to go back to Wynstones. [I]

…Safeguarding has nothing to do with keeping children safe – which is a matter for every responsible adult – and everything to do with locking schools into a control system and creating regulatory obligations that can never be fulfilled. Wynstones was a good safe school with healthy outcomes for the children and very few incidents (compare it to the degree of social, criminal and disciplinary problems at other schools) – parents chose to send their children there at great personal cost; what more evidence is needed of their confidence? [O]

…How this process of closure can be in the best interest of the students attending the school is absolutely ludicrous. It has scattered a strong community of families that made an independent choice of education that we were for the most part happy with, shattered the children's sense of community and thrown them into a sudden and dramatic change that was forced upon us without any consultation or appearance of due care for the welfare of the children. [R]

…Impact on our family: We are seriously looking at moving home to another location as we currently do not have a way forward with local schools being full. [V]

…had the Fellowship been overseeing the management of the school as well as the educational provision, we would never even have been in this position…. …I do lay the ultimate blame for this with the Fellowship, because it is their job to look after the schools, and they were not even present for any of the meetings. Without the schools they have no purpose. [W]

…I can't see that this [closure] is an effective way to improve teaching and learning in any way, shape or form. The trauma and disorientation it creates for a large number of individuals and families has been experienced by us as a total contradiction to any notion of a 'duty of care' that could have led to such a decision. [X]

…I believe that the majority of parents were happy with their choice of school in Wynstones. Most families, to my knowledge, were making lifestyle cuts to pay the fees because they were not well off but really wanted this type of education for their children. Do you really think people would make struggles and sacrifices to send their children to a school which was not safe and caring and nurturing? [Z]

…The closure of the school completely turned our lives upside-down. We had chosen this education and our son had chosen it too, recognising that the curriculum met him on an emotional level as well as intellectually. It fed his imagination as well as his artistic sensibility. [A- II]

…For [schools as] cultural institutions to thrive, they need freedom. People need to be given trust and each and every school needs to evolve organically to become the school that it is destined to become…. In my life, I've come to conclude that so much that comes from above (governmental dictates) has the effect of "dumbing-down", not raising standards. [A-II]

…The parents and children I feel for most are those that have had to relocate (both job and home) from the Xxxxxxxxxx Steiner School to Wynstone's Steiner School – due to one school closure caused by OFSTED – only to suffer another school closure and be thrown into the same turmoil, and uncertainty, once again. [A-II]

…I was shocked and surprised at the closure of the school, especially as it seemed to be due to safeguarding, something with which I have never had an issue. My children have always felt safe and cared for during their time in the school. [A-III]

…A short term closure to get training etc. up-to-date might have been a positive thing for the school, since, as teacher myself, I know it is difficult to get these things done whilst managing the demands of a school. However, this is evidently not a short-term closure for the benefit of the school and the teachers. [A-IV]

THE SCHOOL CLOSURE PROCESS

… It's right that [problems in the school] are highlighted and concerns raised, but does this warrant a school closure and disruption on this scale?… we can only assume that the school was closed following a one-off complaint where the correct procedure wasn't followed through. How can this warrant an entire school closure? [A]

…All the secrecy is not necessary as I have learned more and more what the closure was all about. [C]

… Leaving over 300 students without a school and having other schools to pick up our children at this time of year is totally unacceptable…. Instead of closing us down please just talk to the parent body first as a whole and list your concerns without it all being so secretive. [C]

… I don't question that some things needed to change or improve but to close the whole school is ridiculous! [D]

…My 11 year child has been through hell!…. On the 27th January after a lovely day at school we learned that without any kind of notice we could not take our children back to school. Shocking! [G]

…The closure came as a total shock. There was no prior warning. [M]

…The impact on children throughout the school – whether those too young to understand what has happened, right up to those whose exam schedules have been upset – amounts to a form of organisational abuse. [M]

...The overnight closure of the school was a profound shock which has caused our family, and particularly my son, huge distress and confusion.... The lack of clarity and sense of timescales that I have had have meant I have felt completely disempowered in my ability to give him some kind of coherent narrative around it. [N]

...The sudden and unexpected closure of the school has sent us into a dramatic shift that has had no benefit to our children's welfare. They were happy and progressing in a positive way at the school, had a fantastic and well-supported network of friends and teachers that created a full circle of support that encouraged their sense of self and well being. [R]

...It's been devastating. We've felt isolated and unsupported, completely at sea with very little to navigate by. The tone of letters from the school has gone from being personable to cold and distant and often from people we don't know. [S]

...We feel that closing the school entirely, and so suddenly, is a heavy-handed way of dealing with a specific issue. Our children have always felt safe at Wynstones and we have never had any worries about their welfare while at school. [U]

...Regardless of the reasons for closure, there are numerous, less harmful ways that this action could have been carried out. [V]

...we feel that the punishment has been disproportionate and unfair – particularly on exam-aged children who are not even allowed to contact their teacher. How this would represent a risk to the child's safety is baffling and seemingly beyond any sense of reason. [Y]

...To suddenly close a school, especially one where your child was happy and thriving, I find particularly cruel. [Z]

STRESS AND ANXIETY

...We've had the most stressful month, as have so many other parents, with less than 24 hours notice that school was closing and following that a desperate panic to find alternative schools. [A]

…there are still families who haven't managed to secure a place and the added stress of this on top of the school closing is dreadful. You will have heard that the children taking GCSEs and A-levels are in an even worse situation. [A]

… I have heard from parents whose children are at the school that they have been suffering from anxiety, and some are even not sleeping as a result of worrying about their school. [B]

…I believe that the last months at the school have been extremely difficult for the staff as the tension and stress of working under the close scrutiny of Ofsted has created an atmosphere of mistrust and fear that undermined the cohesion of the teacher body. It seems to have also unnerved the parents and this too has created mistrust. [B]

…Stress and distress. This has been ongoing for the whole family from the moment of the closure. There is huge uncertainty, incredible strain on the children in trying to keep up with their exam work, impacts of isolation from the group, anxiety about exam results and the impact on further education plans for university and 6th form. [E]

… The first week of the closure, my 15 year old xxxxx was unsupervised and walking back and forth across Xxxxxx to meet and study with friends. After 3 days of this s/he was in an anxiety state and suffering panic attacks. There has also been the impact of shock. It's a challenge to my world view to be subject to arbitrary, unaccountable and authoritarian decisions that completely devastate my life and against which I have no recourse. My faith in the government, in the world and in my own judgement has been shaken. The stress has been such that I have signed myself off sick because of it. [E]

…The main issue is my xxxx's anxiety. S/he is in Class 10 with GCSE's only 14 weeks away now…. S/he has been suffering with severe anxiety over this; being sick, not eating, shaking uncontrollable [sic] and crying for hours on end. We are seeking medical advice as s/he has lost about a stone in weight in about three-and-a-half weeks. I will be getting in touch with Teens in Crisis. [F]

…Since the Ofsted report last year the school had already been living in fear, walking on eggshells with the threat of closure looming like a death sentence!! Children were leaving, and the remaining parents were becoming increasingly nervous about what might happen! [G]

…My health is suffering greatly. I am totally stressed out – a bag of nerves. I hope the powers that be who won't let the children take exams don't sleep at night, because I'm not. [H]

…Since the closure…, for the first time in his life, s/he has been having daily screaming tantrums, waking crying in the night, and his/her behaviour has been hard to manage and completely new for him/her – throwing things, hitting, pushing etc. This is obviously enormously distressing for him/her and for me. [N]

…Emotionally they have also been severely affected, going into a depression and my daughter breaking out in a stress-related rash. They have lost their motivation and their joy in life – a very sad thing to witness in children. My daughter is often tearful and was shocked to be told that according to OFSTED the teachers are no longer even allowed to look at them if they see them. [O]

…Our xxxx, who struggles with social skills, is now left at home with nowhere structured to go, we do not want him/her to go to a state school, so we are struggling for things to do with him/her…. All our xxxx is wanting to do is disappear into his/her Sci-fi book world and hide from reality, we are struggling to get him/her to do anything school wise. [P]

…Our xxxx is restless, structureless, friendless and has expressed a sadness and anger at what has happened to his/her beloved school. S/he misses all his/her lessons and teachers, and is finding it hard to motivate him/herself to do anything. [P]

…Negative psychological social and educational impact on our children. [R]

…Our xxxx is anxious about the future of his/her education, shown by an uncharacteristic reluctance to engage in set school work. S/he is unhappy about suddenly losing classmates. [U]

… Impact on the children: To not be able to fulfil experiences that have been looked forward to for years – for example, my xxxx has been planning his/her Class VIII project for many years and my xxxx's wish has been to go to the Olympics…. To have treasured work in progress suddenly abandoned (for example, my xxxx was working on a xxxxxx piece for my birthday and was so distressed that s/he couldn't finish, let alone give me his/her work). [V]

...Impact on me personally: I am self-employed and the financial, mental and emotional stress of suddenly having two devastated two pre-teen children in my full-time care is enormous. My physical and mental health is not in a good place at the moment due to the above.... I am struggling to support the children's emotional needs. I am already at breaking point and am finding it hard to help them cope. [V]

...Emotional: The closure has led to 6 weeks of stress, anxiety, disorientation, de-motivation and confusion for xxxx's and their parents at the most crucial point of their education. [X]

...The shock and the distress on us as parents has been massive – especially as we spent 14 months trying to move to the area, so our son could go to Wynstones, going through a very stressful house sale and purchase.... We were looking forward to finally being settled in the area, when our world came crumbling down. [Y]

...The amount of stress, upset and disruption that it has caused for our xxxx and us as parents, is heart breaking.... ...How hard that is as parents to watch your happy, confidant child, go into despair? [Z]

...[I have a] demanding job and I need to recharge my batteries if I am to perform to the best of my ability with challenging students. ...These last few weeks, I've felt really stretched and by Friday night I've been on my last legs, stumbling through the door, desperate for my bed. [A-II]

...My xxxx has felt very much in limbo, with the uncertainty of whether the school will reopen or not.... S/he doesn't want to go to another school at this late stage in his/her education as s/he has a very good rapport with his/her teachers and doesn't want to have to face getting to know a new environment and teacher. [A-III]

TRAUMA AND LOSS

...the significance of this final year of Middle School and not being able to see it through is heartbreaking for us and the children who were half way through their major Year 8 projects and excitedly fund-raising for their final class trip, when all this happened. [A]

...It's with huge sadness that most of us won't be able to finish Class VIII because we feel we have to take places and settle our children in their new schools. We have no idea if and when Wynstones will reopen. [A]

…My xxxx was very upset, lost and without a structure that s/he needs. I was upset as I did not know / was not given options for my xxxx, and we were unable to contact the teachers – how ridiculous! [C]…The school's closure has been really difficult for our entire family. My children have been shocked and traumatised – my oldest child has heard people talking and now thinks s/he is not good enough academically… Sh/e is angry and bored and missing his/her friends. [D]

… We are all devastated and heartbroken by the closure. [D]

… Loss. The close-knit community which we and our children are a part of at Wynstones has been blown to pieces. Children who have been close friends are scattered. All the extra-curricular enrichment activities, such as morning singing, choir, crafts, PE and school trips, are lost. All their connections with the other classes, the teachers and support staff, all their routines are lost. All the fundraising work they have put towards the class XII trip is lost. There is no closure, and no celebration of the time they have spent together. We are in a grieving process at the same time as trying to create some kind of structure and stability in the face of huge bureaucratic obstacles. [E]

…My heart is broken but I will never give up on Steiner education! [G]

…Hearing my daughter say how much she misses her teachers, morning singing and how much she wants to sing in Gloucester Cathedral in the summer. How much she wants to be with the class, finish a whole lifetime of Steiner Education in an appropriate fashion with a festival at school as it should be…. I realise that she has been in the right place. [H]

…Our xxxx misses her friends and s/he is missing out on education. S/he is very anxious about the situation. S/he loves her school and is frightened about it being permanently closed. This closure is doing her psychological harm. [I]

…With the continuing closure of the school, three of my xxxx's closest friends have decided to transfer to a different school. She cried all evening when she heard that her three close friends were going to go to a different school. [I]

…This is such a sad time for her. She has been at the school for 6 years, and it is the only school she has been to. She values the non-competitive approach in the Steiner classroom, and when she recently did two 'trial days' at another school she was shocked at the insensitivity of the teachers in comparing the children's work. She is a very able pupil, but hates competition and comparison and shaming. She also really appreciates the arts and crafts and music facilities and teaching at Wynstones, which are way above the standard of the other (private) school she might have to move to. [I]

…The situation the last few weeks has been horrible for my family. First the shock, how this can happen? Do we live in a dictatorship where the state can decide a school needs to close without clear communication with the parents? [J]

…My heart is just broken, we can't communicate with my son's teacher [who] has been with us for 6 years, all our school/education plans for the future years shattered. [J]

……This has caused a huge disruption to our family life and our children's sense of security. [K]

…The child who is now having to move on has not had an opportunity to properly mourn the loss of a school which was central to her life since a toddler. The other child is in a state of limbo…. [K]

…My xxxx is missing his/her friends and his/her teacher. Sh/e is missing the routines and activities which form such an important part of his/her life. [M]

…I feel huge sadness, and outrage, on [my xxxx's] behalf, that his/her brave first steps into the world beyond home have been so suddenly tripped up. The fact that s/he has suddenly not been allowed to see the caregivers s/he had formed an attachment to, and not been allowed any kind of coming together to explain what is going on, has made the experience genuinely traumatising – like a confusing bereavement. [N]

…The closure of the school has been catastrophe for us on many levels. On a practical level the children are bereft of the education that we had invested in, they have lost their friendship group, their confidence and their faith in school. [O]

…This closure has helped to take a great love of learning out of our child in a matter of weeks, this is so sad and upsetting for us. [P]

...Impact on the children: Unable to see, speak or hear from their teachers – whom they have been with for up to 7 years – it is like there has been a mass death. [V]

...suddenly, without warning, it's all been taken away! No chance to discuss or explain, no chance to see his/her teacher, whom s/he has been with for the past 6 years, no chance to collect his/her belongings, say his/her goodbyes. All the work s/he has put into her studies, just whipped away from him/her. No chance for him/her to go up to Upper school in September, like s/he was looking forwards to. Can you imagine what that must be like for a 1x year old?... ...This has caused us tremendous grief. [Z]

...My xxxx, my whole family (including grandparents) [were] completely distraught when we heard the news. It was absolutely heart-breaking. To have your child come home happily chatting about their school day and then to hear (from another distraught parent) at gone 7 pm, when I was just tucking my child into bed, that the school was closed and s/he just couldn't go back the next day... it was unbelievable, a kick in the gut... I don't know how my xxxx managed, I barely coped myself... up all night crying... [A-IV]

ANGER AND OUTRAGE

...Angry with the school that they did not have a parent meeting that week of closure to inform us right away of what is going on and why the school has been closed. [C]

...Having had one child go through Steiner education who is now in his/her second year at Xxxxxxx University and is being hailed in many quarters as being one of the brightest stars they have ever had, I simply can not tolerate that Steiner education in this country be hounded out of existence by small-minded bigots who have no clue as to what they are talking about. [G]

...My xxxx and I have now got to leave our home once again and move to Xxxxxxx so that he can go to Xxxxxxx school.... I am a Steiner parent and together we will run the gauntlet kicking Ofsted in the teeth to get to class ten wherever we have to go!!! [G]

...We are angry and annoyed, it seems like such an overreaction from the D of E [sic], but sadly it also seems that this sort of homogenisation is the way things are going. [K]

...I feel a terrible grief and anger that s/he has had to go through this complete wrong-footing and I fear for the impact it will have on his/her ability to make confident, trusting starts in his/her education in the future. The emotional cost of it is enormous. [N]

…I remain furiously angry…. [O]

…The suddenness with no reasonable explanation has left my xxxx sad and my xxx, incredibly angry. My xxx expressed wanting to kill him/herself two days after closure as s/he was so distraught. Their main issue is that they (nor I, to be honest) can understand WHY such extreme action was required. [V]

…Our overall experience has been one of grief turning towards anger. The decision and enactment of the decision felt brutal, unjust and out of proportion. [A-I]

FEELING UNSAFE, AND UNSAFE CHILDREN

…None of the 30 to 40 families we know have any first-hand knowledge (let alone adverse experience) of safeguarding issues in general, let alone the specific issues that have ostensibly got OFSTED's alarm bells ringing. None of them felt unsafe before…. S/he never felt unsafe at Wynstones. [L]

…But [the children] sure as hell feel unsafe now: 1) having found alternative school places at institutions they had ruled out (shunned?) in recent years, maybe with good reason; or 2) having failed to find alternative school places; and/or 3) now in desperation planning to tackle home schooling (which they had previously ruled out, probably with good reason). [L]

…We both work full time and therefore it has been very difficult for them to be constructively engaged – the result is that they are often hanging out in town without us knowing where they are and what they are doing – not the best thing for a 10 and 12 year old who should be in school. [O]

…The Ofsted report says that students were at 'significant risk of harm'. We think the class 10 students have been actually harmed by the closure of the school. [T]

…By attempting to avoid potential safeguarding issues, Ofsted has created actual safeguarding incidents. [V]

…In the beginning, due to no other option and time to plan alternative arrangements, we have had to leave our children on their own on occasions. [V]

EXAMINATIONS [PREPARATION]

Xxxxx and all his/her class mates have been seriously disadvantaged by this closure as they are facing these extremely important exams and are now not even sure that they will have a school to return to. I believe also that their course work can only be marked by Wynstones teachers and that may mean that they cannot sit the exams at another school if Wynstones does not re-open. [B]

… [My children] have missed, and are still missing, critical teaching time in the run-up to their exams. I don't know what the outcome will be, but I expect their grades to drop. We are talking with the universities and 6th forms they want to move on to, but there is a strong possibility that their future education will be compromised. My xxxx is unlikely to be able to take all the GCSEs s/he has been studying for, and may only be able to sit 5 of the original 8. My xxxx will not be able to complete the Practical Endorsement for his/her xxxxxx A-Level again, with potential consequences for his/her future education. [E]

…I wonder if this was the right move for exam students who are struggling enormously to find a place to go….it's been over 3 weeks now of no support for them. No one would plan this for their children. No one could possibly think this is acceptable. AND I am very upset!!!! [H]

…As a parent having to spend every waking hour trying to come up with solutions for my xxxx finishing his/her year 13 education with some qualifications. Making pleas to other schools to take him/her for A-levels and getting nowhere (in Xxxxxx). Trying to find tutors for him/her. Calling up his/her Art School to make dispensation for maybe not having ANY A-LEVELS. [H]

…Trying to find somewhere for our xxx to take his/her exams was very time consuming and very frustrating. Educational because our xxxx has missed lots of quality teaching time, half way through his/her GCSE year! [T]

…Our xxxx is concerned that the break in his/her education will adversely affect his/her A-level results and therefore his/her chance of going to university. S/he is disappointed that his Wynstones journey from kindergarten through to class 12 will not now be completed. …We, as parents, have found it hard to find a suitable alternative for our xxxx to complete his/her A levels (which s/he should be sitting this summer) at such a late stage in the 2 year programme. [U]

…With one xxxx 4 months away from sitting her A-Level exams and another xxxx 4 months away from sitting his/her GCSE's, this immediate closure and ban from any contact with their teachers (and a total lack of any guidance or support of contingency from the DfE for supporting students facing the most poignant moments in their education careers to date) is negligent, inexcusable and totally unnecessary. [X]

CHILDCARE, WORKING PARENTS AND FINANCIAL EFFECTS

… It has also been a very difficult and trying time for parents who work and who have had to find child care for their children. This has also incurred extra expense for them. [B]

… It has been difficult for myself and my husband because we both work so we were put in the position of suddenly having to find childcare – it has been a nightmarish juggling act and I question how 'safe' the children have felt being carted from pillar to post – often with people they don't know very well. I have had to drastically cut the hours I work also. …I have had to take time off work and reduce my working hours to manage the administrative nightmare of trying to find viable options for my children to take their exams (my children are in Class xxx and xxxxx, doing GCSEs and A-Levels in just a couple of months). I have literally been working on this full time for a week and it's not done yet. I haven't managed – and don't want – to enrol them full time into other schools so have had to make time to support their learning at home. This means I will be losing significant income – around £2,000. [E]

…Now I need to find a new school for my children as I am a working parent and I can't home school. Local schools are full, the local authority is not willing to help. The schools that are not full are worried about taking in children they have not been trained to take exams because that may affect their ofsted grade… it is a nightmare. [J]

…The childcare issues are very difficult. My business as a xxxxxxxxxx is difficult as I am having to juggle childcare around seeing patients…. my wife will possibly have to give up work in order to look after her [whilst] we await the fate of Wynstones and / or await the appeals process trying to get her into a state primary school. [K]

…We have had to find many hours of childcare, which has impacted on us professionally, financially and emotionally. [M]

…There is also a financial cost – I'm now scrambling to try and find something else for him to go to so that the impact of starting then stopping is not so great, and struggling to find anything I can afford to pay for; if the changes in his behaviour continue I may need to find some kind of therapeutic input for him to try and make sense of the experience. [N]

…It is difficult as parents to be working and balance time for our son at times where he should be at school. We think we are all still shocked that this is happening to our school… [P]

...Practical [negatives] because we had to spend a lot of time working out how to find and arrange tutors, arrange transport, talk to other schools, etc. etc., with limited help from Wynstones (hands tied behind backs) and almost no help from the educational authorities. [T]

...As well as loss of income, we are having to pay for private tutoring and to register privately for some exams. I estimate that the final cost of getting both children through their exams will be in the region of £5,000 (although we will not be paying school fees to Wynstones, so some of this will be recouped). [E]

...Negative psychological financial and social impact on us as parents. [R]

...Financial [negatives] – extra costs of tutors, extra travel, loss of earnings because of the time spent on the above logistics instead of working. Also now expecting extra costs for exams because we missed the 21st Feb deadline. Stress – including worry and anger – from all of the above – for us and our xxxx. [T]

...The school closure has caused us added expenses for travel and tutors while we attempt to provide some interim schooling for our children. [U]

...To compensate for the loss of friends and structure, I have been trying to organise playdates, study dates, outings, etc. All of these activities and planning take time out of my work life – which means loss of income.... Lost income for work that I have had to turn down as I am now looking after the children. [V]

...Cost: carrying on from the above, the cost incurred to us as a family due to this closure – and to ensure that the xxxx's have the best chance of sitting their exams and succeeding educationally (isn't that what the DfE and OFSTED are meant to be supporting?????) will amount to many thousands of pounds by the end of June. This is one area for which I would appreciate redress. [X]

...With so much uncertainty as time has gone on, we have resorted to homeschooling, using tutors. My wife and I both work full time. I leave the house at 7 am and return at 6 pm. It feels like I am coming home to begin another work shift at the moment. Coordinating home schooling with tutors and x other families that are in the same boat, with cancellations, re-jiggings, explanations to tutors that have never taught to a Steiner Curriculum before, just what we are looking for, all takes time, as do payments and settlements of payments between parents. [A-II]

…s/he was finally really happy and finally considered it to be 'his/her' school… everything I had went into that school…we have been living with xxxxxxxx just to be able to attend Wynstones, because it was the very best thing for my son/daughter… Now s/he is at home, still, nearly a month and a half later…. No purpose or direction. [A-IV]

LASTING HARM

… I'm in no doubt that this has done lasting harm to young people's lives and that of their families too. [A]

…The long-term impact of a school she loved being at and felt safe at and then was ripped away for her, will be immense. I feel this will take a long time to get over and many hours of therapy! [F]

… The impact of this will be felt for many years to come for all of the children that have had their beloved school so violently taken from them! Ultimately, whatever the DfE's intention here, it will be the children that suffer for this in the long term. [F]

…Wynstones may need to make changes, but we feel that the effects on those students has been unnecessarily harsh and may set many of them back by at least a year. [T]

…Lack of process; students and parents will carry forward for the foreseeable future a sense that there was no suitable process, acknowledgement of relationships built over years, hand-over, completion of teaching and learning tasks. Shocking. [X]

…A child (albeit nearly a teen) left alone at home for hours at a time?? Is this really preferable to sending him/her to the school s/he loved?? It has affected my own teaching practice, as I am forever reminded of the injustice and indescribable upset of the closure of Wynstones…. Who can sleep sound any more? Who can relax and enjoy life?? [A-IV]

OFSTED AND THE DEPARTMENT FOR EDUCATION (DfE)

… I hope there's a way forward to expose the injustice and prejudice wielded by Ofsted and DfE on our school and on Steiner education more broadly. [A]

…The DfE must be held accountable for their end too. It would be helpful and politically correct to have a date and time when they will review and give us a date when we can reopen…

How about getting some urgency with you DfE! You have hundreds of students without a school and forcing them to attend other schools and change their lives. [C]

…This closure was ridiculous, and not [being] given any notice was very unsettling and unprofessional by the DfE…. The DfE needs to think before they close a school of our size and 80 years of being a well attended Waldorf school. There could have been other options and methods than this…. [C]

… The inspectors kept his class in for an entire break time – to ask them if they felt safe at school. [My xxxx] just could not understand it. [D]

… The closure of the school by the DfE single-handedly traumatised far more children and parents in one fell swoop than school could ever have done. Would it not have been more constructive and less damaging if Ofsted were to say – yes, there is a problem – how can we help you to sort it out? [D]

… I am shocked by the lack of accountability and the refusal by the DfE to take anyresponsibility for their decision to close the school and for the consequences of this. It is hard to believe that they have made absolutely no provision and offered absolutely no support for our children, and when challenged on this – I have complained to the DfE, Ofsted and my MP – there is no acknowledgement that any of it has anything to do with them. [E]

… The DfE have had no regard for any of Wynstones' pupils in the [throes] of their exams; no contingency plan has been put in place and the teachers have not been allowed to send out work or have any contact with students to support them at this time. [F]

… How can the DfE justify closing a school due to a so-called Safeguarding issue that only involved a few members of staff and some pupils on the one hand, but create an even bigger problem, with regards to the well-being of all pupils, parents and staff, on the other? (What about the safeguarding of children who are likely to be left at home alone while parents go to work)? How legal is this process? How accountable can the DfE and Ofsted be over this situation? [F]

… There has been minimal support for parents trying to cope with their children and having to work. The school have their hands tied by the DfE as not allowed to send work home. What responsibility do the DfE have towards parents and children? Apart from telling us we have 20 days to find alternative provision! This is an [appalling] situation for anyone to be in, but as a parent of a child about to take her GCSE's this is an unforgivable action on the part of the DfE. [F]

…This bullying organisation have [sic] ruined our school. I believe that this is part and parcel of the fascist regime we are under in this country to rid itself of any education system which produces free-thinking open-minded individuals instead of the 'cannon fodder' raised in Dickensian institutions that pass for state schools! [G]

…The Department of [sic] Education have shown absolutely no responsibility towards these children. They appear not to care two figs about the educational prospects of the children taking exams. They should let the school open as an exam centre. [H]

…[the sudden closure the school]… just seems like a heavy-handed action by a body who wish to see Steiner schools abolished for idealogical [sic] reasons. When safeguarding issues arise at other schools, even very serious issues or scandals, the schools are never closed down by Ofsted. On reading the Ofsted report, my sister-in-law, who is a supply teacher in state schools, said 'All schools are like that'. [H]

…Many lives are being damaged by the heavy-handed action of Ofsted in closing Wynstones, in circumstances which would never lead to the sudden closure of other schools, which are not suddenly closed down over safeguarding irregularities. I have not heard of [a] similar drastic Ofsted action, but I have often heard of much more serious safeguarding scandals in schools, which of course were not closed down. [I]

…We have received no explanation from the DofE, they claim they are protecting our children but they obviously couldn't care less. The Ofsted report says nothing of substance showing no understanding (or even try [sic]) of the Waldorf curriculum. It is insulting the way they talk about teachers and parents…. [J]

…OFSTED's inspections (usually unannounced) have been hanging over the entire institution for months like the sword of Damocles. The resulting fear among staff was entirely rational in so far as the only solution is compliance. With silly cosmetic changes? Jargonistic groupthink? No matter, compliance is required. Conversely, opposition or counter-attack is futile (example: King's Langley, now shut). [L]

…We feel that we are dealing with faceless bureaucracy – the DfE seems to be completely oblivious to the turmoil and worry that has been unleashed…. If Wynstones was guilty of placing children at 'risk of significant harm', then the DfE is guilty of actual abuse. The hypocrisy is astonishing. [M]

…The DfE, in dragging its feet over making a decision about the school's action plan, is effectively destroying the school. Worried parents are naturally looking for alternative settings for their children as they feel compelled to break the deadlock of uncertainty. [M]

…Together [OFSTED and the Department of Education] have seriously damaged our children in the name of a very dubious 'safeguarding' procedure which has nothing to do with children's safety. They should be made to pay the full costs in reparations to the parents, the school and the children, although of course the real cost they have inflicted by tearing a community apart and ruining children's live cannot be measured. [O]

…I am also aware of schools such as St Edwards in Oxford where there is a known paedophile working at the school who was under investigation – yet OFSTED chose to take no action. I know this first hand from a parent there. Do OFSTED think they know better than parents, children and teachers? Just on the basis of a 2-day visit and shuffling some paperwork while interrogating teachers with their GESTAPO questions? It's absurd! Parents are responsible for their children, NOT state apparatchiks. [O]

…I remain furiously angry with OFSTED, the Department of Education [sic] and the mindless bureaucratic regime behind it which is controlling, faceless, unaccountable, devoid of common sense and cannot be challenged. [O]

…We asked [our local Gloucester MP] about the legality of Ofsted closing a school so suddenly, we asked if there was a bullying attitude from this government towards Steiner schools in general, we asked whether this government was targeting Steiner schools aiming to discredit and close them down as soon as they got any chance to do so. Our MP has so far not replied to a second email sent out to him asking these questions again, we sent this out a few weeks ago. [P]

…I have seen no justification to close the school in such a manner and am disgusted by the Department of Education [sic] for the lack of support offered to the students and parents to guide them in their education to the point that I feel that what they have done and how they have done it must be verging on the edge of criminal….I sincerely hope there is an inquiry as to how the Department of Education [sic] could possibly see their action as justified, suitable, legal or even reasonable. [R]

…As far as I'm aware closing a school with immediate effect is unprecedented and [a] deeply inappropriate action when the welfare of children is at the heart of the matter. Withdrawing all contact between teachers and parents/pupils is extraordinarily harsh and, in my opinion, wrong. [S]

…We feel strongly that Ofsted / DfE have failed the GCSE and A-level students with this heavy-handed action in their exam year. [T]

…We feel that closing the school entirely, and so suddenly, is a heavy-handed way of dealing with a specific issue. Our children have always felt safe at Wynstones, and we have never had any worries about their welfare while at school. [U]

…The school closure comes at a particularly bad time for those pupils sitting GCSE and A-level examinations this summer, but this does not appear to be an important factor in Ofsted's judgement. [U]

…Short-sightedness: That the DfE/OFSTED could close a school, cut off an exam process and assume (if they did) that students would 'find another school' is blinkered and absurd. They would know, as well as any head teacher or teacher, that different schools work with different exam boards, are at different stages in their curricula, have different emphasis, quality of teaching etc. Our two xxxx's are needing to shift – in some cases – exam boards, course materials and even drop subjects altogether due to the incompatibility of one school's GCSE and A-Level curriculum over another. This is one of the most shocking and absurd outcomes of the DfE's decision. [X]

…Undermining the DfE's and OFSTED claims for education – a decision like this flies in the face of supporting education and a diverse approach to education in this country. It is a draconian decision made with little sense (or care) for the consequences for this decision for students in their exam years (let alone for the other students). [X]

…Not enough can be said about the totally [sic] irony of closing a school on 'safeguarding' grounds and creating the degree of trauma that that decision has generated as a result. Staggeringly irresponsible on behalf of OSTED and the DfE. [X]

…I believe Ofsted/the DfE must be held accountable for their actions, which have caused so much stress and heartache to children and carers, and everyone associated with the school. They have surely caused much more harm than they have supposedly prevented…. We are very upset that Ofsted have deemed it necessary to cause so much stress and uncertainty to so many children and carers in the name of protecting their safety. [Y]

…The lack of warning and preparation was shocking, as has been the very prolonged response from the DfE to the school's attempts to both care for the children and move towards reopening. It seems that no provision was made to assist the pupils in gaining places elsewhere. It has been an extended period of limbo which has felt unnecessary and distressing. [A-I]

…We have felt powerless as we have witnessed the disproportionate power of a government body to dramatically alter the life of a community of individuals who are more than capable of making sound decisions for the well being of their children. This did not in any way feel a protective gesture for our young person, but quite the opposite, causing sadness and anxiety. [A-I]

…Had OFSTED identified issues that were of concern and needing improvement and then set out to help the school to work towards making these improvements in a constructive way, then I might be able to talk about a positive dimension to the work of OFSTED. [A-II]

…With such a high emphasis on 'safeguarding' we allow the lowest (basest) qualities of mankind – abuse of children – to dictate the agenda; if too much in time and resources are dedicated to this, there is little energy left to devote to the essential.

Once 'Safeguarding' established its place as "Top Trump", it became very difficult to question its position; who doesn't want our children's safety to be put as: of the highest importance? Thus was OFSTED's power as the supreme judge of every educational standard, cemented and made unquestionable. [A-II]

SOME 'POSITIVES' FROM THE CLOSURE

…I think the closure gave xxxxx this chance to discover his own capacity to manage himself. [B]

… The only possible positive of the schools closure has been that the teachers and admin staff have had time to complete training and paperwork. [D]

…Not having to travel in a minibus to school from Xxxxxx. My daughter being able to practise her cello more often…. Seeing how resilient and how adaptable the whole class are and how they are continuing with their studies at home without any help from their teachers, doing their absolute best. [H]

…I really can't think of anything positive about the stressful situation we are going through, maybe only that it made me realise how much [I] value my children to be able to attend a school like Wynstones. [J]

…I see very little real positive impact of the schools closure, other than the financial relief of not having to pay fees. [K]

…The only clearly positive aspect I can see is a small one. This is the financial impact on those families that have now in desperation found places at state schools (for their ex-

Wynstones pupils). So they now no longer have to pay the school fees. A minor collateral benefit perhaps, certainly not a source of joy or security. [L]

…Another remote but possible consequence would be tighter school administration involving clearer lines of responsibility (retaining a flat salary structure, and pigs will fly). [L]

…On the positive side, my child and I have made contact with children and parents beyond our immediate circle, though still within the school community. The efforts of many parents to create play dates, activities and childminding opportunities has been inspiring. Most importantly, the sense of community and mutual support, be it practical or emotional, has helped to slightly mitigate the worry and uncertainty we are all enduring. [M]

…the closure has given the school an opportunity to get up to speed with its safeguarding procedures and other aspects of the Independent Schools Standards. [M]

…The only positive thing that has occurred with the closure is how everybody involved in Class 8 (that is our xxx's class) has come together more over these past few weeks than we have noticed in our three years at the school. This has brought a great feeling of togetherness for parents and children at this difficult time, very positive as a support network for us all. [P]

…A very positive aspect of the closure is that it forced us to make a move and get our children into Xxxxxx school as soon as we could. As we'd already put an application in for a trial at Xxxxxx for one of our xxxx's late last year, we had a foot in the door. [Q]

…It is a relief to be free from all the uncertainty. My child has had the rug pulled from under her and while this is traumatic it requires strength of spirit to move forward in new ways. [S]

…a possible positive outcome, though too late for us, is if Wynstones and other Steiner schools, review their commitment to GCSEs. Perhaps the current GCSE curriculum, with its focus on teaching content rather than understanding, are incompatible with Steiner education, which at its best teaches understanding and the joy of learning. [T]

…the way that the Class 10 parents pulled together and helped each other, using WhatsApp for communication, has been wonderful. There are a few particularly shining lights amongst them, but everyone has been involved. [T]

…At best, a rude awakening for the school management to some of the poor communication experienced in the last year. [U]

...The <u>only</u> positive aspect of the school closure on our family has been the financial relief of not having to pay school fees. [V]

...I think to a certain extent the school needed a wakeup call in both the way it is run (trustees), but also to us the parents... [W]

...For us as parents the one positive has been the strength of the community coming together and us becoming an ever-growing part of that. Long term there may be positives as we look at alternative schooling options (none of them state school)... [Y]

...We have been encouraged to work with other parents in the class group to find other options for our young people's education and to share our grief. [A-I]

...An interesting and positive effect for our xxxx was that it made him/her look and take action in what s/he wants to do after school. This focused him/her in a way that exams have not done over the years...I believe [this] is proof of the education s/he has had at the school [and] how it motivates youngsters to learn and take responsibility for their own destinies. [A-III]

...In terms of the school, it has given an opportunity to bring the staff together to look at how they can better serve each other and how to restructure the school to enable it to better serve the diversity of students needs and create an education that is rich in its content and believes. [A-III]

TELLING THE WORLD

...The distress which Ofsted and the DfE have inflicted on our children at such a crucial juncture in their development and schooling should not be allowed to happen without the wider public being made aware of this injustice, a call for accountability and transparency around why such a drastic decision can be taken with no warning and absolutely no support from the agencies who have placed us all in this vulnerable position. [A]

WHAT CAN WE DO? – A FUTURE FOR THE SCHOOL?

…what next? What can we all do to expose this appalling injustice and be heard more publicly? I used to be a press officer and I was wondering if you've been in contact with Richard Adams or any of the education editorial team at The Guardian as this strikes me as something they might be prepared to investigate. [A]

…This temporary closure is likely to kill off Wynstones, because many pupils are moving to different schools so that their education is not interrupted for an indeterminate period. If Wynstones reopens, it might not have enough pupils to be viable…. Wynstones might be fatally damaged by having lost too many pupils in the interim to be able to stay afloat. [I]

…It looks like the school may not re-open now, if it is closed then this would be such a travesty. [K]

…The school's closure leaves us in a quandary. What other Steiner school will take him? Can we afford to send him there: probably not. In any case, will the next Steiner school shut its doors on us mid-stream? [L]

…If the school is forced to close because of financial starvation, then all the good work being carried out to improve the school will have been in vain. This will be an act of sheer educational vandalism – the like of which I never thought could be perpetrated by a taxpayer-funded institution in a supposedly free country. [M]

…All we want is for the school to re-open… we don't want another school… there is no other Steiner school for her age that we can get her to… we can't afford to move, and I don't want to leave my job. [A-IV]

AFTERWORD

Questioning Inspection

Kevin Avison

*Former Senior Executive Adviser to the
Steiner Waldorf Schools Fellowship*

During one of his many stays in the USA, Albert Einstein was teaching at Princeton. As was required by the university authorities, he set his final-year students an exam. The teaching assistant, to whom he had handed the exam papers, was puzzled:

'Dr Einstein, is there some mistake? These questions seem to be identical to those you gave to the same group last year.'

'Yes, yes', Einstein replied, 'they are the same'.

Emboldened, the assistant asked, 'But how can you give the same exam to the same class two years in a row?'

'Ah, you see, the questions are the same, but the answers have changed.'

Ofsted takes the opposite course to Einstein's: the questions keep changing, but the answers they expect are the same. In other words, they continually revise and tinker with their framework, but expect 'compliance' as the answer, which can then be forced into the straight-jacket of four grades, or outcomes – 'Inadequate', 'Requires improvement', 'Good', or 'Outstanding' – portmanteau terms into which an enormous content of variety can be untidily packed.

Compliance to basic standards may not sound like a bad thing. Children are, after all, compelled by law to attend 'full-time education' (albeit 'at home or otherwise'; bearing in mind that provision for five children aged five years and over is obliged to register as a school and so be inspected). But while fundamental conditions for welfare, health & safety and effective provision for learning might contribute to the betterment of children and young people, a continuous, and increasing, welter of regulation, much of it driven by here-today-gone-tomorrow politicians, suggests different priorities. Given that schools in general are the safest places for children, safer than their homes, we have to wonder as does Richard House, whether 'safeguarding' has become the regulatory equivalent of the Dangerous Dogs Act. Official reviews of safeguarding rules have concluded that their complexity, in fact, results in greater hazard. Yet simplification moves ever further away. Ofsted's role is, of course, not to make the regulations, but it is to enforce them.

In doing so, Ofsted claims to be 'independent and impartial', and the myth of its independent impartiality is what education ministers rely on when selecting their evidence, and claiming success for their policies. In reality, however, since school standards are beyond obvious, and certainly not the absolutes they aspire to be, inspections involve almost limitless scope for interpretation and the influences of prejudice, whether deliberately chosen, or, more often, dependent on the interior of what passes for the official mind, including group think.

The truth of the matter is, as Professor Frank Coffield has pointed out, that Ofsted is a government department, subject to the whims and failings of politicians of all shades, not to mention those of Chief Inspectors, who are appointed by the incumbent Secretary of State. There may be no better illustration of a lack of checks and balances in our constitution, and of its ever-present danger of 'elective dictatorship' (to use Lord Hailsham's words) than a body such as Ofsted. Significantly, when Ofsted is found seriously wanting, as happened at a September 2018 Public Accounts Committee (PAC) hearing, the response was to double down on what Ofsted was already doing, while preparing to introduce yet another tweaked version of its inspection framework. The slew of news about Ofsted tackling 'failing schools' after that PAC hearing is unlikely to be co-incidental.

We could envisage a different way to inspect schools, and we do not have to travel far to find a better, less confrontational approach. Scottish HMIE and, to a lesser degree, Estyn in Wales, although not perfect, present viable alternative models. The name 'Estyn' itself is evocative, since it means 'to reach out, or extend', as in providing help and support. In both nations the emphasis is on giving advice and helping schools to improve. Elsewhere, as Professor Saville Kushner mentions in his Foreword, there are countries (he references Sweden and New Zealand) which have even more effective methods of promoting positive school development. It should not be a matter of surprise that evaluation in those settings is directed towards learning, and thus real and sustainable change. If schools are about learning, what they need is encouragement to be institutionally engaged in learning, developing better ways to respond to the emergent future within growing children and in a world in which 'the answers to the questions', those facing humanity, are transforming.

Ofsted serves to suppress change because its institutional pretence is one of knowing the answers even before the questions have been asked. When Michael Gove, a former Education Secretary but speaking in another context, expressed his personal frustration with the words, 'the nation is fed up with experts', he blew the gaff on a deep-seated, dirty secret about much that happens in politics. He placed himself squarely on the grounds of a rather counter-productive and disreputable tradition in English life, that which chooses to turn away from the hard work of thinking, and ignores the need to seek for evidence, in favour of a determination for the approval of conventional prejudice: 'I don't need to learn: I know what I think already'.

I cannot speak for the detail of the Wynstones case itself – Richard House's thesis has done that, and there clearly is a case answer. The vital issue here arising from the Wynstones inspection and many similar situations is, how can we move towards a much more thorough, educational ethos capable of fitting individuals and their society for a world of change? Ofsted is a failed answer that clings on by forcing schools into the mould of its own misshapen likeness. Education is change in process and process for change: lifelong learning.

It's time for new answers.

INDEX